151731

ISRAEL'S SURE TOMORROW

A Prophetic Odyssey

ISRÆL'S SURE TOMORROW

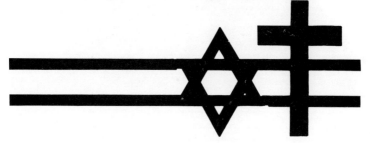

JAMES BLACKSTONE

ISBN 0-88965-075-6

BUENA BOOKS
A division of Horizon House Publishers
Box 600, Beaverlodge, AB, Alberta, Canada TOH OCO
Drawer AA, Cathedral City, California 92234

Printed in the United States

TABLE OF CONTENTS

Part I
ISRAEL'S SURE TOMORROW

                                                            Page
I. Confusion in Interpreting Prophecy   13
II. The Apostle Paul's Burden for Israel............   21
III. The Prophecy of Israel's Great Day   35

Part II
GOD'S COVENANTAL RELATIONSHIP WITH ISRAEL

IV. Israel's Covenant Through Abraham............   57
V. Israel's Covenant Through Moses..............   73
VI. Israel's Covenant Through David   85
VII. Israel's Captivity and Return   95
VIII. Israel's Destiny Revealed Through Daniel   107
IX. Israel's New Covenant in Christ   123
X. God's Lament Over Israel   139
XI. Conclusion and Appeal for Prayer   148

APPENDIX A. Prophecy and Fulfillment.........   156

APPENDIX B. Comments on Revelation 20:1-9
   Regarding the Millennium   173

APPENDIX C. Comparison of Differing Views
   on Certain Prophetic Events Between
   W.E. Blackstone and J.H. Blackstone   178

APPENDIX D. Scripture Texts Cited   182

BIBLIOGRAPHY   186

To my dear wife,
Jean
who has faithfully shared
in all the work
of the ministry.

FOREWORD

God has placed a growing sense of responsibility upon me to write this book on one of the most specific and important prophecies in the New Testament. The implications of this prophecy have been either overlooked or misunderstood by those who have dealt with it so that the true intent and full meaning of the writer, the Apostle Paul, has seldom, if ever, been explained. There are many scholars who have written books debating the issues which concern the nation of Israel and the Second Coming of our Lord Jesus and I would not presume to write another book to throw into their debate. This one is different.

Being heir to a home background of strong pre-millennial teaching and with a highly respected grandfather, William E. Blackstone, who is widely known as the author of the book, *Jesus is Coming*, I have always been looking for the blessed hope of our Lord's return. Through over forty years of pastoral ministry, I have read and studied the writings of many scholars on the subject of eschatological teaching and certainly have not been able to deal with every prophetic passage in detail or to discuss at length every verse that bears on this subject.

My concern is to show what God has promised (through Paul's prophecy in Romans 11:25,26) to do for Israel as a nation before Jesus returns and what this will mean to the Christian church. Then in order to understand the full scope of God's dealings with this chosen nation more fully, we shall consider His covenant relationship with Israel through her two thousand years of history from Abraham to the coming of the Messiah and the New Covenant sealed in His precious blood.

Our Lord prophesied that "Jerusalem would be trodden down of the Gentiles until the times of the Gentiles be fulfilled" and His words are being literally fulfilled today. In Romans chapter 11, St. Paul reveals a mystery "that blindness in part is happened to Israel until the fullness of the Gentiles be come in." A careful study of this chapter shows clearly that the interplay of Jew and Gentile is God's plan of accomplishing His work of grace and of calling all of His own to salvation in this world. He has promised to remove the partial spiritual blindness from Israel and, through their personal belief, so many of them will be grafted back into the same olive tree into which the Gentiles have been grafted that it will be like "receiving" their "fullness" as "life from the dead." What joy this will bring to the Christian church throughout the world and what a wonderful testimony to God's grace before a world that is ripe for judgment!

Through my study of the Scriptures, I became convinced of several vital truths that influenced my conclusions as to the final events preparing for the return of our Blessed Lord.

1. Abraham's seed even after they were in the land of Canaan did not receive the promises but confessed that they were strangers and pilgrims on the earth and looked for a better country—that is a heavenly country.

2. The Lord Jesus did not intend to have a worldly kingdom, like the world empires of Babylon, etc., but to rule over a worldwide kingdom of subjects who have been born again and commit their hearts to Him in absolute surrender and loyalty. His Kingdom will last forever, not just 1000 years.

3. The Lord Jesus accomplished the six great works of Daniel's prophecy within the 70 weeks (490 years) determined upon the chosen people and the holy city, not in 69 weeks plus 1900 and more years plus one week.

4. Ever since the cross of Jesus, God's purpose was to make of Jew and Gentile one new man in Christ and He has preserved the Jews as a distinct people only that when the full number of Gentiles have been brought into salvation, He may at the last pour out His grace and bring the unbelieving nation to salvation.

5. The Mosaic law was temporary until the Messiah should come. It was done away when the New Covenant, sealed in the blood of Christ, was confirmed by Jesus, with believing Israel, including believers of all nations; therefore, the law, which God says could not give life, certainly will never be reinstituted with Israel to govern human society in this sin-cursed world.

6. Paul plainly teaches in I Corinthians 15 that at the rapture, death, which is Christ's final enemy, will be vanquished bringing the end when Christ will deliver up the kingdom to the Father that God may be all in all.

7. It is significant that neither Peter in II Peter 3, nor Paul in I Corinthians 15 allow for an earthly millennial kingdom; in fact, after Pentecost, none of the disciples mention the restoration of the kingdom to Israel.

Having presented what I believe to be God's truth revealed in His Holy Word, the final purpose of this book is to call Christians everywhere, as well as Jews, to pray for Israel. Let us pray, not primarily for her material prosperity and peace with the Arab nations, but that she will confess the awful guilt of continued rejection of the sacrificial love of her own Messiah before it is too late and the door is shut when the Bridegroom comes for His Bride, the Church. Today is the day of salvation, *not after Jesus comes,* and we must pray earnestly now that God will remove the judgment of partial spiritual blindness, which He has kept for 1900 years upon Israel and will pour out upon them the spirit of grace, calling them to repentance and to eternal salvation through faith in Jesus, their Messiah.

I trust that the reader will continue to read this short book to the end and be led to pray earnestly for the salvation of Israel NOW, EVEN BEFORE JESUS COMES!

Part I

ISRAEL'S SURE TOMORROW

CHAPTER I

Confusion in Interpreting Prophecy

NEARLY 2000 YEARS AGO, Israel missed her great day of visitation when her Messiah came to Jerusalem as the Saviour and King of the Jews. He looked down upon the beloved city from where He stood on the Mount of Olives and wept tears of compassion as He foresaw the terrible destruction that would come upon the nation. "Behold, your house is left unto you desolate," He told them. But He also said, "Jerusalem shall be trodden under foot of the Gentiles until the times of the Gentiles be fulfilled." Did His words of prophecy concerning the city come true? Certainly they did, and we, in our generation after 1900 years, are the ones who have seen it come to pass. Can anyone deny that this was under God's providence and through His sovereign control of the nations? And since this prophecy of Scripture has been so wonderfully fulfilled, we should give careful study to another prophecy which is revealed by Israel's Messiah through His commissioned apostle, Paul, in Romans chapter 11, which is yet to be fulfilled. There He says,

For I would not, brethren, that ye should be ignorant of this mystery lest ye should be wise in your own conceits; that blindness in part is happened to Israel, until the fullness of the Gentiles be come in. And so all Israel shall be saved: as it is written, there shall come out of Zion the Deliverer, and shall turn away ungodliness from Jacob: For this is my covenant with them, when I shall take away their sins.

In writing on the subject of prophecy, it is obviously impossible to give an adequate and full interpretation of every text in Scripture that deals with future events, nor do I propose to attempt this. My concern is primarily with important basic issues presented in the Scripture where the interpretation of the texts are clear and will determine the resulting system of prophetic understanding. This is where so much disagreement and confusion have resulted even among those who have fully accepted the inspired Scriptures as the only authority of faith and doctrine. The differences usually do not pertain to the gospel of salvation, the doctrine of the Trinity, the person and work of Jesus Christ or the work of the Holy Spirit. They have rather to do with such truths as the covenant and promise to Abraham, the spiritual application of Old Testament promises and prophesies, God's plan for the Jewish nation, the seventieth week of Daniel, chapter 9, the Tribulation Period and the Millennial Kingdom. Our interpretation of certain basic Scriptural truths, which we will consider, will determine the system of prophetic teaching which we will adopt. The differing views of prophecy ought not in themselves to divide true believers into different camps, nor should they sever the bonds of fellowship within the church, the Body of Christ.

NEW TESTAMENT INTERPRETS OLD

I believe that the Old Testament, as well as the New Testament, is the word of God and that "All Scripture is given by inspiration of God and is profitable for doctrine, for reproof, for correction, for instruction in righteousness" (II Timothy 3:16). Furthermore, I believe that since the New Testament was given us after the fullness of the revelation of God in the

Person of His Only Son, our Lord, we must allow the New Testament writers to interpret the fulfillment of the Old Testament prophecies as the Holy Spirit led them. This is most important. The New Testament writers not only had been given the promise of the Holy Spirit, who would guide them into all truth (John 16:13) and would bring to their remembrance all things whatsoever He had said unto them (John 14:26), they also had Jesus Himself as their instructor in understanding what the prophets had said concerning Him.

> And beginning at Moses and all the prophets he expounded unto them in all the Scriptures the things concerning Himself (Luke 24:27). And He said unto them, these are the truths which I spake unto you, while I was yet with you, that all things must be fulfilled which were written in the law of Moses, and in the prophets, and in the psalms, concerning Me. Then opened He their understanding that they might understand the scriptures (Luke 24:44,45).

This surely should convince us that the New Testament writers give us the correct interpretation of Old Testament prophecies as to their fulfillment and we must be very careful that our views do not conflict with theirs. It is essential for us to allow the Holy Spirit through the New Testament writers to teach us how the words of the Old Testament prophets are fulfilled, rather than to place upon those words our own interpretation of how they must be fulfilled and then demand that only by satisfying our interpretation of fulfillment can God really be true to His Word.

This was the reason for Israel's failure to know the time of God's visitation among His people when Jesus the Messiah came to His own nation. They were blind to everything except a literal fulfillment of a messianic hope that promised deliverance from Roman tyranny and would lead to world domination by Israel. They could not understand that their Messiah would come as the Lamb of God to deliver them from the bondage of sin and to establish His Kingdom that would include believers from every race and nation and would last forever.

There are two quite different systems of teaching on the subject of eschatology that are widely held among evangelical

Christian teachers today. The pre-millennialists teach that the Lord Jesus Christ, about seven years after He comes to rapture the church out of this world to meet Him in the air, will return to earth and then reign here in an earthly kingdom for a thousand years before the final day of resurrection and judgment. On the other hand, the a-millennialists teach that the reign of Christ has been going on during the church age while He has been gathering His subjects into His Kingdom and that when He comes again the general resurrection will take place, including the rapture of all believers, followed by the judgment and the everlasting Kingdom. There is also a third group, the post-millennialists, who teach that the second coming of Christ will not precede but will follow a still future one thousand year period of world peace and prosperity under worldwide acceptance of the Christian gospel, but it does not seem necessary for my purpose at present to discuss this view which is not widely accepted.

I recognize that there are differences even among those who hold the pre-millennial position, such as pre-, post- or mid-tribulation rapture of the church or extreme dispensationalism but in general let us accept the three groupings of pre-, a-, and post-millennialists.

In examining the teachings of the pre-millennialists and a-millennialists, we discover that there are not only minor differences of interpretation of certain passages of Scripture, but that some of these differences are both contradictory and very important. For example, in the interpretation of the vitally important prophecy given in Daniel 9:24-27, the pre-millennialists believe that Jesus did finish the six accomplishments and that He is the One who was to confirm the seventy-sevens of years (490 years) and that it is the Anti-Christ who makes a covenant with Israel for seven years which he breaks in the midst of the seventieth week. The a-millennial believe that Jesus did finish the six accomplishments and that He is the One who was to confirm the covenant with many during the seventieth week. To say that Jesus did not finish what is prophesied in Daniel 9:24, if He really did accomplish it, is quite a serious mistake. And it is just as serious a mistake to say that the Anti-Christ will make a covenant of death with Israel and will break it by stopping the temple sacrifices if Jesus the Messiah made the

New Covenant of life with believing Israel over 1900 years ago and stopped the sacrifices by giving Himself on the cross as the supreme once-for-all sacrifice for sin. It does make a tremendous difference how we interpret scripture!

There are many such verses or passages of scripture that we could cite, but what is most disturbing is not that there have been differences but that scholars on both sides seem to have looked at scripture through "systemized" lenses so long that they cannot study the Word of God without trying to fit the verses into their particular system. There are some Bible-believing scholars who discuss the issues with an attitude of "my system is right—yours is wrong" and who do not seem willing to explore areas where both may be wrong!

This attitude was expressed in a letter from a prominent radio ministry in which the writer said, "We do not believe that it is incumbent upon us to harmonize these contradictory views. How can you harmonize black and white? We do not believe it is our business to try to harmonize them, certainly not to the extent of changing or altering what God has said about His people, Israel." Now certainly no Bible-believing scholar would ask someone who differed from him to change or alter what God has said about His people, Israel, or about anything else. God's Word stands true. It has not changed with the centuries and we dare not alter it.

BOTH RIGHT AND WRONG

It is not what God has said but the differing interpretations by fallible men and women of what God has said that have caused the wide divergence of eschatological teaching. And surely, the true scholar should be concerned to try to understand why God, the Holy Spirit, who is the true teacher of the believer should have allowed individuals as well as large groups of Christians to arrive at such opposing interpretations. They study the same Scriptures, they have the same teacher, the Holy Spirit, they both pray for wisdom and guidance at learning the truth, they believe the same doctrines concerning Jesus as to His birth, ministry, atoning sacrifice, death and resurrection but concerning prophecies about Israel, the Return of Christ and the millennium, they are poles apart.

Something must be wrong somewhere. But is it possible that God permitted this divergence in teaching to occur over-ruling the mistakes of men? Could God have had a purpose in allowing such a division within the Body of Christ? Might it be that in order to carry out His purpose of restoring Israel to her homeland, He used the support of pre-millennialist Christians who emphasized the physical and material promises of God to the Chosen People and believed in a yet-future hope for the nation of Israel? On the other hand, lest it should be forgotten that salvation has always been, is now and always will be by faith alone and that the middle wall of partition between Jew and Gentile was broken down when Jesus died on the Cross, did He use the a-millennialists, who emphasized the spiritual promises to Israel but ignored the promised future blessing upon the nation?

Both the pre-millennialists and the a-millennialists have been partly right and partly wrong. God has used both groups to maintain and carry out His great purposes. He has finally brought His chosen people back to the land as a nation and it is high time that Christians should study God's Word again to learn what God's real purpose is in dealing with them in this way. Certainly this event is in fulfillment of the prophecy of Jesus, the Messiah, who said, "Jerusalem shall be trodden down of the Gentiles until the times of the Gentiles be fulfilled" Luke 21:24.

ROMANS 11:25

But it also prepares for the fulfillment of another New Testament prophecy given in Romans 11:25,26 and here is where we find serious differences of interpretation: "For I would not, brethren, that ye should be ignorant of this mystery lest ye should be wise in your own conceits; that blindness in part is happened to Israel, until the fullness of the Gentiles be come in. And so all Israel shall be saved."

The pre-millennialist reads the prophecy as though it says the blindness remains until the church is complete and the rapture takes place; then the blindness will be removed. The a-millennialist reads it correctly, "until the fullness of the Gentiles have come in" but argues that the word "until" does not require the removal of the blindness after the point of time is reached.

Strange that the clear Word of God written by the inspired Apostle Paul should be so misunderstood! But the pre-millennial system of eschatology requires a distinction between the salvation of the church, the bride of Christ, and the later salvation of national Israel when they see Jesus. It requires Israel under the Old Testament law again, with another temple and priesthood, with Jesus sitting on a literal throne in Jerusalem reigning over the nation of Israel and also over the nations of the world for 1000 years. It wouldn't do to have national Israel saved by God's mercy and grace with the salvation Paul is talking about and grafted back into the same root or vine into which the Gentile believers have been grafted for 19 centuries. It wouldn't do for Israel nationally to become a part of the believing church that is caught up at the rapture when Jesus comes again so the nation would not be here on earth to continue into the earthly millennium. So, with their colored glasses they read the words, "...until the full number of Gentiles have come in" as though it were the completion of the church and the rapture had occurred. Then Israel will be saved. But look again; what does God's Word actually say?

The a-millennialist regards Israel nationally as having been rejected or cast away although the remnant was and still is being saved. Consequently, it doesn't fit into their system to have God deal with Israel on a national basis bringing them to salvation. They, therefore, go to the extreme of forcing a strange meaning on the word "until" as though it expresses a point of time that is to be reached but does not involve a change in the blinded condition of the nation of Israel. But common sense reveals how strained this interpretation is. Suppose a mother punishes her son for something he has done by requiring him to stand in the corner with his face to the wall until four o'clock. Would we expect that he would still have to stay there after the clock strikes four? Of course not! Four o'clock would mean the end of the punishment. Certainly, when God placed Israel under the awful punishment of partial blindness and said it would remain on them until the full number of Gentiles were come in, we are to expect that in His divine mercy the judgment would be lifted.

What would have been the point of Jesus saying, "Jerusalem shall be trodden under foot of the Gentiles until the times of the Gentiles be fulfilled" if Jerusalem would continue to be trodden under their feet after the times of the Gentiles are fulfilled? It would make utter nonsense! And the present existence of the nation of Israel today does make nonsense if such an interpretation were forced on the word "until" in the prophecy of Jesus.

KEY WORD: UNTIL

So in Paul's prophecy in Romans 11:25, he has been talking about a judgment of partial blindness that was placed on them until the full number of Gentiles have been grafted into what began as a Jewish church. He plainly indicates the point of time involved in the word "until" to be the ingathering of the full number of Gentile believers. Notice that Paul does not say until the ingathering of the fullness of *all* believers, *Jews* and *Gentiles*. Note, too, that there is no reason from this passage to equate the ingathering of the full number of *Gentile* believers either with the eschatological culmination or with the return of Christ for His church.

We will see why the meaning of the word "until" is so important in interpreting this prophecy as we study the entire eleventh chapter of Romans in greater depth. But for the present, we have found that the pre-millennialist reads Romans 11:25 with a mind prejudiced by his interpretation of Old Testament promises of a salvation for Israel separate and distinct from the church with a future Jewish kingdom over which Messiah reigns for 1000 years. On the other hand the a-millennialist reads the same prophecy in Romans 11:25 with his mind prejudiced against any hope for national Israel to enjoy the blessing and mercy of God. Both of these groups are missing the true teaching of the prophecy. How wonderful it would be if they both could read the same passage without any prejudice and arrive at the same interpretation of the actual Word of God as written! Is God's Word really so difficult to understand? Why can't we try to understand what the inspired Apostle really says and what he really means by his words and come to agreement on a New Testament prophecy which both groups maintain is very important? Then together the church of Jesus Christ might unite in praying that God will remove the blindness from Israel so they will behold the wonder of His grace and believing, they will be grafted back into the Church of our Lord and Saviour.

CHAPTER II

The Apostle Paul's Burden For Israel

IN ORDER TO UNDERSTAND what Paul is revealing in the eleventh chapter of Romans it is necessary to read through the three chapters consecutively, beginning with chapter nine:

1. I tell the truth in Christ, I am not lying, my conscience also bearing me witness in the Holy Spirit,

2. that I have great sorrow and continual grief in my heart.

3. For I could wish that I myself were accursed from Christ for my brethren, my kinsmen according to the flesh,

4. who are Israelites, to whom pertain the adoption, the glory, the covenants, the giving of the law, the service of God, and the promises;

5. of whom are the fathers and from whom, according to the flesh, Christ came, who is over all, the eternally blessed God. Amen.

6. But it is not that the word of God has taken no effect. For they are not all Israel who are of Israel,

7. nor are they all children because they are the seed of Abraham; but, "in Isaac your seed shall be called."

8. That is, those who are the children of the flesh, these are not the children of God; but the children of the promise are counted as the seed.

9. For this is the word of promise: "At this time I will come and Sarah shall have a son."

10. And not only this, but when Rebecca also had conceived by one man, even by our father Isaac,

11. (for the children not yet being born, nor having done any good or evil, that the purpose of God according to election might stand, not of works but of Him who calls),

12. it was said to her, "The older shall serve the younger."

13. As it is written, "Jacob I have loved, but Esau I have hated."

14. What shall we say then? Is there unrighteousness with God? Certainly not!

15. For He says to Moses, "I will have mercy on whomever I will have mercy, and I will have compassion on whomever I will have compassion."

16. So then it is not of him who wills, nor of him who runs, but of God who shows mercy.

17. For the Scripture says to Pharaoh, "Even for this same purpose I have raised you up, that I might show My power in you, and that My name might be declared in all the earth."

18. Therefore He has mercy on whom He wills, and whom He wills He hardens.

19. You will say to me then, "Why does He still find fault? For who has resisted His will?"

20. But indeed, O man, who are you to reply against God? Will the thing I formed say to him who formed it, "Why have you made me like this?"

21. Does not the potter have power over the clay, from the same lump to make one vessel for honor and another for dishonor?

22. What if God, wanting to show His wrath and to make His power known, endured with much longsuffering the vessels of wrath prepared for destruction,

23. and that He might make known the riches of His glory on the vessels of mercy, which He had prepared beforehand for glory,

24. even us whom He called, not of the Jews only but also of the Gentiles?

25. As He says also in Hosea:
    "I will call them My people, who were not My people, and her beloved, who was not beloved."

26. "And it shall come to pass in the place where it was said to them, 'You are not My people,' there they will be called sons of the living God."

27. Isaiah also cries out concerning Israel:
    "Though the number of the children of Israel be as the sand of the sea, The remnant will be saved.

28. For He will finish the work and cut it short in righteousness, because the Lord will make a short work upon the earth."

29. And as Isaiah said before:
    "Unless the Lord of Sabaoth had left us a seed, we would have become like Sodom, and we would have been made like Gomorrah."

30. What shall we say then? That Gentiles, who did not pursue righteousness, have attained to righteousness, even the righteousness of faith;

31. But Israel, pursuing the law of righteousness, has not attained to the law of righteousness.

32. Why? Because they did not seek it by faith, but as it were, by the works of the law. For they stumbled at that stumbling stone.

33. As it is written:

"Behold, I lay in Zion a stumbling stone and rock of offense, and whoever believes on Him will not be put to shame."

Romans, Chapter 10

1. Brethren, my heart's desire and prayer to God for Israel is that they might be saved.

2. For I bear them witness that they have a zeal for God, but not according to knowledge.

3. For they being ignorant of God's righteousness, and seeking to establish their own righteousness, have not submitted to the righteousness of God.

4. For Christ is the end of the law for righteousness to everyone who believed.

5. For Moses writes about the righteousness which is of the law, "The man who does those things shall live by them."

6. But the righteousness of faith speaks in this way, "Do not say in your heart, 'Who will ascend into heaven?'" (that is, to bring Christ down from above,)

7. or, "'Who will descend into the abyss?'" (that is, to bring Christ up from the dead).

8. But what does it say? "The word is near you, even in your mouth and in your heart" (that is, the word of faith which we preach):

9. that is you confess with your mouth the Lord Jesus and believe in your heart that God has raised Him from the dead, you will be saved.

10. For with the heart one believes to righteousness, and with the mouth confession is made to salvation.

11. For the Scripture says, "Whoever believes on Him will not be put to shame."

12. For there is no distinction between Jew and Greek, for the same Lord over all is rich to all who call upon Him.

13. For "whoever calls upon the name of the Lord shall be saved."

14. How then shall they call on Him in whom they have not believed? And how shall they believe in Him of whom they have not heard? And how shall they hear without a preacher?

15. And how shall they preach unless they are sent? As it is written:

    "How beautiful are the feet of those who preach the gospel of peace, Who bring glad tidings of good things!"

16. But they have not all obeyed the gospel. For Isaiah says, "Lord, who has believed our report?"

17. So then faith comes by hearing, and hearing by the Word of God.

18. But I say, have they not heard? Yes indeed:

    "Their sound has gone out to all the earth, and their words to the ends of the world."

19. But I say, did Israel not know? First Moses says:

    "I will provoke you to jealousy by those who are not a nation, I will anger you by a foolish nation."

20. But Isaiah is very bold and says:

    "I was found by those who did not seek Me; I was made manifest to those who did not ask for Me."

21. But to Israel he says:

    "All day long I have stretched out My hands to a disobedient and contrary people."

Romans, Chapter 11

1. I say then, has God cast away His people? Certainly not! For I also am an Israelite, of the seed of Abraham, of the tribe of Benjamin.

2. God has not cast away His people whom He foreknew. Or do you not know what the Scripture says of Elijah, how he pleads with God against Israel saying,

3. "Lord, they have killed your prophets and torn down Your altars and I alone am left, and they seek my life."

4. But what does the Divine response say to him? "I have reserved for myself seven thousand men who have not bowed the knee to Baal."

5. Even so then, at this present time there is a remnant according to the election of grace.

6. And if by grace, then it is no longer of works; otherwise grace is no longer grace. But if it is of works, it is no longer grace; otherwise work is no longer work.

7. What then? Israel has not obtained what it seeks; but the elect have obtained it, and the rest were hardened.

8. Just as it is written:

   "God has given them a spirit of stupor, Eyes that they should not see and ears that they should not hear, To this very day."

9. And David says:
   "Let their table become a snare and a trap, A stumbling block and a recompense to them;

10. Let their eyes be darkened, that they may not see, And bow down their back always."

11. I say then, have they stumbled that they should fall? Certainly not! But through their fall, salvation has come to the Gentiles to provoke them to jealousy.

12. Now if their fall is riches for the world, and their failure riches for the Gentiles, how much more their fullness!

13. For I speak to you Gentiles; inasmuch as I am an apostle to the Gentiles, I magnify my ministry,

14. If by any means I may provoke to jealousy those who are my flesh and save some of them.

15. For if their being cast away is the reconciling of the world, what will their acceptance be but life from the dead?

16. For if the first fruit is holy, the lump is also holy; and if the root is holy, so are the branches.

17. And if some of the branches were broken off, and you, being a wild olive tree, were grafted in among them, and with them became a partaker of the root and fatness of the olive tree,

18. do not boast against the branches. But if you boast

remember that you do not support the root, but the root supports you.

19. You will say then, "Branches were broken off that I might be grafted in."

20. Well said. Because of unbelief they were broken off, and you stand by faith. Do not be haughty but fear.

21. For if God did not spare the natural branches, He may not spare you either.

22. Therefore, consider the goodness and severity of God: on those who fell, severity; but toward you, goodness, if you continue in His goodness. Otherwise you also will be cut off.

23. And they also, if they do not continue in unbelief, will be grafted in, for God is able to graft them in again.

24. For if you were cut out of the olive tree which is wild by nature, and were grafted contrary to nature into a good olive tree, how much more will these, who are the natural branches be grafted into their own olive tree?

25. For I do not desire, brethren, that you should be ignorant of this mystery, lest you should be wise in your own opinion, that hardening in part has happened to Israel until the fullness of the Gentiles has come in.

26. And so all Israel will be saved, as it is written: "The Deliverer will come out of Zion and He will turn away ungodliness from Jacob;

27. For this is my Covenant with them, When I take away their sins."

28. Concerning the gospel they are enemies for your sake, but concerning the election they are beloved for the sake of the fathers.

29. For the gifts and the calling of God are irrevocable.

30. For as you were once disobedient to God, yet have now obtained mercy through their disobedience,

31. even so these also have now been disobedient, that through the mercy shown you they also may obtain mercy.

32. For God has committed them all to disobedience, that He might have mercy on all.

33. Oh, the depth of the riches both of the wisdom and the knowledge of God! How unsearchable are His judgments and His ways past finding out!

34. "For who has known the mind of the Lord?
    Or who has become His counselor?"

35. "Or who has first given to Him and it shall be repaid to him?"

36. For of Him and through Him and to Him are all things, to whom be glory forever. Amen.

Some have suggested that these three chapters are a parenthesis in the Apostle's thought and have no relation either to chapter eight or chapter twelve. However, it is much more reasonable to recognize that there is a natural flow of thought from chapter eight to chapter nine. In the early part of this letter to the Romans, Paul had declared that he was "not ashamed of the gospel of Christ for it is the power of God unto salvation to everyone that believeth, to the Jew first and also to the Greek" (Romans 1:16). On his first missionary journey, preaching in the synagogue in Antioch in Pesidia, Paul after much opposition from the Jews said, "It was necessary that the Word of God should first have been spoken to you: but seeing ye put it from you, and judge yourselves unworthy of everlasting life, lo, we turn to the Gentiles" (Acts 13:46). To the Jew first and then to the Greek was God's plan. Then in Romans, Paul shows that both the Gentiles who were without the law as well as the Jews, who had the law but couldn't keep it, were sinners before God. "For all have sinned and come short of the glory of God" (Romans 3:23). The only way that sinners are made righteous is by accepting through faith the righteousness of Christ who died for us while we were yet sinners. "For the wages of sin is death: but the gift of God is eternal life through Jesus Christ our Lord" (Romans 6:23). He proceeds to show that as we are called to righteous living we find our victory over sin in Christ, and in chapter eight declares the presence and power of the Holy Spirit to keep us eternally in the love of Christ. What a difference it makes when a person believes and is saved by the gracious calling of God. And what a tragedy for those who judge themselves unworthy of everlasting life and are separated from God for all eternity. Thinking of the blessings which Israel had forfeited by their unbelief, Paul solemnly vows that it is true that he has "great heaviness and continual sorrow in his heart" (Romans 9:2), and he even declares, "For I could wish myself accursed from Christ for my brethren, my kinsmen according to the flesh" (Romans 9:3). In an earlier letter written to the Christians in Thessalonia, Paul had said of the Jews that they had "both killed the Lord Jesus and their own prophets and have persecuted us; and they please not God, and are contrary to all men: forbidding us to speak to the Gentiles that they might be saved, to fill up their sins alway: for the wrath is come upon them to the uttermost" (I Thessalonians 2:15,16). No wonder his heart was deeply moved as he thought of what was coming upon them and of what blessings they were missing by refusing Jesus, their Messiah. So chapter 9 begins with this strong avowal of his heavy sorrow and his deep concern for Israel, his nation.

It is very important to keep in mind that Paul has the nation of Israel upon his heart and that he is referring to the unbelieving nation in this whole section of Romans 9-11, except when he specifies the elect believing remnant.

UNBELIEVING ISRAEL

In chapter 9:4,5, he expresses the covenantal relationship which Israel had enjoyed with God who had chosen her to be a special people. Yet in spite of her privileges as a nation, she was guilty of the awful sin of unbelief and her leaders had encouraged the Roman authority to put Jesus, God's Son, to death upon the cross.

Therefore, in Romans 9:6-9, Paul shows that Israel's unbelief had not nullified God's Word, for the true children who were counted as the seed of Abraham were those who had the faith of Abraham. Isaac was the child of promise, given to Sarah and Abraham because "she judged Him faithful who had promised" (Hebrews 11:11). Thus we have Isaac, the son of Abraham by Sarah, born of faith and accepted as the true seed in contrast to Ishmael, the son of Abraham by Hagar, the child of flesh who was rejected. Again, there is a contrast drawn between Jacob who was chosen and Esau who was rejected on the basis only of God's sovereign election. We are taught by this that even Jacob's seed must be part of the election in order to be counted the true seed of Abraham having his faith. God claims the right to have mercy on whom He will have mercy, and Paul's answer to those who object to God's right to choose is given in his challenge: "Who art thou that repliest against God?" It is far better to listen and respond to the gracious invitation given by God that "whosoever will may come" and "him that cometh to Me, I will in no wise cast out," than to stumble over the apparent difficulty of understanding His electing grace and consequently refusing to come to Him in faith, believing His love for you.

Of course, it is difficult for us human beings to understand completely the ways of God with sinful men. We know from Scripture:

1. that the wages of sin is death (Romans 6:23).

2. that God did not create man a sinner but he became a sinful being by free choice, refusing obedience to the will of his Creator (Romans 5:12).

3. that death came upon all men because all have sinned (Romans 5:12).

4. that salvation is only by faith in Jesus the Messiah and Redeemer who died for our sins and rose again (Acts 16:31).

5. that the door has been opened for Jew and Gentile to believe and call upon the Name of the Lord (Romans 10:11-13).

6. that there is no unrighteousness with God, but He has the right to have mercy on whom He will have mercy (Romans 9:14,15).

In Romans 9:24-29, Paul quotes from the Old Testament prophets Hosea and Isaiah to support the fact that God had in mercy called His people, not from the Jews only, but also from the Gentiles. His quotation from Isaiah also tells us that out of the vast number of the children of Israel only a remnant will be saved. However, both Hosea and Isaiah foretold better days that would come to Israel because the remnant had been spared through the days of apostasy and judgment upon the nation. It is very important to take note of this because God uses the same method of sparing a remnant when it might appear that He had cast away His people in 70 A.D. This points toward future blessing for the nation when the punishment or judgment is over.

In Romans 9:30-33, Paul sums up his discussions by showing that ethnic or national Israel has not attained to righteousness because they sought it not by faith but by works of the law. When Jesus the Messiah came to Israel, He was the precious stone which the nation refused to build upon and which, therefore, became a stumbling stone to them and a rock of offense. How tragic that their eyes were so blinded that they refused to look upon the glory of God in the face of Jesus, their Messiah, and have as a nation despised Him through these nineteen centuries!

As we continue on in our brief survey of these two chapters, we find Paul again expressing in Romans 10:1 his earnest desire that Israel might be saved. Surely we must recognize this to mean that he longed for the Jews to accept the wonderful gospel of salvation that brings justification and righteousness by faith to any and all who believe.

In Romans 10:2-5, he points out what is basically wrong with the Jews' effort to attain righteousness, readily admitting that they do have a zeal for God. They were still trying to attain to their own righteousness by strictly observing the law rather than by accepting the righteousness of God, which He had provided at infinite cost through the death and resurrection of His Son, our Lord Jesus Christ. By instituting the Aaronic priesthood, the temple ritual and the sacrificial system for His chosen nation, God had shown them that the law could not save a person from his sins. He needed an atoning sacrifice and this now was provided through the sacrifice of the Lamb of God on the cross of Calvary. Through the prophet Jeremiah, God had declared that since Israel had broken the covenant of law, a New Covenant would be made with His people:

> But this shall be the covenant that I will make with the House of Israel: After those days, saith the Lord, I will put My law in their inward parts and write it in their hearts; and I will be their God and they shall be My people. And they shall teach no more every man his

neighbors and every man his brother saying, Know the Lord: for all shall know Me from the least of them to the greatest of them, saith the Lord: for I will forgive their iniquity and I will remember their sin no more (Jeremiah 31:33,34; Hebrews 8:10-12).

But when Jesus sought to ratify that covenant with the nation, which He had made in the upper room with His disciples, He was rejected and they refused to believe on Him.

In Romans 10:6-17, the way of salvation is made plain for both Jew and Greek. It is a matter of believing the word of faith which is proclaimed in the Word of God. Even from the earliest record of human history, righteousness has only come to those who have truly believed God. Read again the great chapter of faith in Hebrews 11 and see how from Abel down through Israel's history, those who truly believed God were accepted as righteous. Since the cross of Christ was set up on Golgotha, the same message of faith has been preached:

That if thou shalt confess with thy mouth the Lord Jesus and believe in thine heart that God has raised Him from the dead thou shall be saved. For with the heart man believeth unto righteousness and with the mouth confession is made unto salvation (Romans 10:9,10).

Paul emphasizes the right of anyone to enjoy this salvation if only he will believe. Whoever believes and whoever calls on the Name of the Lord will be saved. The same Lord over all, Jew and Greek, is rich unto all who will come to Him. The good news of salvation must be preached because faith comes by hearing and hearing by the Word of God.

Then finally, in chapter 10:18-21, he faces the question of Israel's unbelief and apparent rejection by God. He asks, "Haven't they heard?" and answers with a quotation from Psalm 19 that the Word has gone out even to the ends of the world. But did not Israel know? In 10:2 he had already said that Israel had "a zeal of God but not according to knowledge." So instead of answering the question here he quotes the words of Deuteronomy 32:21, a prophecy given through Moses of how God would deal with the unbelieving and stubborn nation to bring them back to Him. Note that Moses was speaking to Israel as a nation when he says that God

will provoke you to jealousy by them that are no people and by a foolish nation I will answer you (Deuteronomy 32:21).

He then quotes from Isaiah, who speaking for the Lord said,

"I was found of them that sought me not: I was made manifest unto them that asked not after me" (Isaiah 65:1).

Clearly, these prophecies by Old Testament prophets were referring to those who would have the message of redemption brought to them, the Gentiles who were not seeking the truth but to whom the glad tidings of salvation were preached.

In contrast to the Gentiles who were receiving the Gospel, Israel was a disobedient and gainsaying nation to whom God stretched out His Hands pleading with them all day long. That day has continued on and on for nineteen centuries and still God stretches out His Hands to Israel! In II Corinthians 6:2, Paul emphasizes the fact that "now" is the accepted time: "Now is the day of salvation." Surely the God of Israel would not hold His nation under judgment for nineteen centuries and allow the "day of salvation" to slip away without permitting them to participate in that "day" with the judgment of blindness removed. This is what makes Romans chapter 11 so important in understanding national or ethnic Israel's place in God's plan of bringing salvation to the world. Let us move on then to consider exactly what the apostle has said and understand the prophetic significance of this vitally important chapter.

CHAPTER III

The Prophecy of Israel's Great Day

W HEN WE CONSIDER the failure of Israel as a nation to be the witness of righteousness which God chose them to be, we begin to learn one of the most important lessons that the Lord is teaching us. That lesson is that it is impossible for a sinner to establish his own righteousness. Our human effort cannot save us from sin, only true faith, believing in the Saviour who loved us and gave His life for us. But Israel as a nation stubbornly refused to believe. Instead of believing on Him when He came, they sent Him to Calvary crying out, "Crucify Him! Crucify Him!, His blood be on us and on our children"; "We have no king but Caesar!" Then when the nation of Israel officially through the Sanhedrin condemned the preaching of the resurrection and the good news of forgiveness of sin through the crucified and risen Saviour and began to severely persecute the believers, especially those who preached the gospel to the Gentiles, they filled up the cup of their iniquity and brought upon themselves the wrath of the Almighty. As the Jews continued to resist the gospel of Christ and at the same time the door was opened wide to the Gentiles who received the message of life with gladness, the question naturally arose in the minds of many, "Hath God cast away His people?"

CONTINUED EXISTENCE OF ISRAEL

This is the question with which Paul continues immediately after he has quoted from the Old Testament scriptures the declaration of God's patience in continuing to stretch out His hands to a disobedient and gainsaying people. But now has God's patience finally been exhausted? Has their sin of unbelief and rejection been so great that He at last has cast them away and will no more deal with them as His chosen people? God forbid! That would have denied God's declaration spoken centuries before through the prophet Jeremiah concerning the continuance of Israel as a nation (Jeremiah 31:36,37).

In Jeremiah 31:31-35, the prophet had foretold the establishment of a new covenant with the house of Israel to replace the old Mosaic covenant which they had broken. Then without any indication that there would be a problem regarding their acceptance of the New Covenant, Jeremiah adds two important verses, 36 and 37:

> If those ordinances (of nature) depart from before Me, saith the Lord, then the seed of Israel also shall cease from being a nation before Me forever. Thus saith the Lord, if heaven above can be measured and the foundations of the earth searched out beneath, I will also cast off all the seed of Israel for all that they have done, saith the Lord (Jeremiah 31:36,37).

This is a promise binding upon the God of Israel and it guarantees the continued existence of ethnic or national Israel as long as our present world system endures. In a remarkable way God has kept His word in spite of the terrible judgment He brought upon the nation in 70 A.D. using the armies of the Roman Empire. That generation paid an extremely high price for the overflowing cup of iniquity but He kept His word through the long centuries of dispersion among the various nations of the world and from each generation there has been a remnant of believers. Israel was preserved without a homeland, without a government, without a united language, without a temple, and without an army through many periods of repression and even persecution until today she is strong and vital and becoming more and more self-sufficient. God gave His solemn word through Jeremiah 2500 years ago and has faithfully kept it.

Looking back over the centuries from the beginning of the captivity to the present, it seems almost impossible for God to prove true to the various prophecies concerning Israel that were uttered in His Name. Jeremiah had prophesied that the exile of Israel from the homeland would last for 70 years and then there would be a restoration with the captives returning from the nations where they had been scattered. God waited until the 69th year of captivity and then used Cyrus to overthrow the Babylonian empire. That very year He moved upon Cyrus to issue a decree that the Jews should return to Jerusalem and rebuild the temple of the Lord (Ezra 1:1). How amazing are God's ways!

Around 590 B.C., Jeremiah had also made this significant prophecy concerning the continuance of Israel as long as the ordinances of nature remained.

But around 538 B.C., Daniel was given the prophecy by an angel that seventy weeks (490 years) were determined upon the people and the city of Jerusalem "to finish the transgression and to make an end of sins and to make reconciliation for iniquity and to bring in everlasting righteousness and to seal up the vision and prophecy, and to anoint the Most Holy." He also prophesies the destruction that would follow upon the nation.

APPARENT CONTRADICTION

Here are two apparently contradictory prophecies—the one by Jeremiah that Israel shall last as long as the ordinances of nature endure; the other by Daniel that after 490 years from the decree to rebuild Jerusalem, war and destruction will come upon the city and sanctuary. How can they both be fulfilled?

Remember that God had promised Abraham that He would bless all the nations of the earth through his seed and Paul

37

makes it very clear in Galatians 3:16 that it was not through his physical seed, the nation of Israel, but through the Seed, which is Christ. So when Jesus died on the cross He finished what had been prophesied by Daniel. He made an end of sin, made reconciliation for iniquity. He brought in everlasting righteousness and anointed the Most Holy. (See chapter VIII—Israel's Destiny Revealed Through Daniel.) He also made peace between Jew and Gentile, breaking down the middle wall of partition, abolishing the enmity between them, even the law of commandments (Ephesians 2:14-17). He began to build His Kingdom which would be both world-wide and everlasting, composed of subjects from all nations. The law of Moses was abolished which was the foundation of the nation of Israel and the New Covenant promised by Jeremiah was confirmed with all who would believe, both Jews and Gentiles in one body. Israel nationally was no longer needed to accomplish God's work of salvation— that work had been finished by Jesus, the Saviour, and the Jewish nation in 70 A.D. was conquered by the Romans and became a scattered people. By their fall salvation had come to all Gentile nations. It appeared then that God had forgotten His chosen people and His promise that they would continue as a nation as long as earth's ordinances endured.

But no, God has not forgotten them. He has preserved the nation through nineteen centuries, allowing them their own traditions and distinctive heritage separate from the Gentiles, in spite of their rebellion and continued unbelief, while at the same time He has always invited and encouraged any to come to Him if only they will believe. And now in this exciting century He has driven Israel out of the nations into their homeland where He will yet bring them to repentance and faith in their Messiah. This must be done before Jesus comes bringing judgment upon the unbelieving world and cleansing this world system by fire (II Peter 3). Thus, He will fulfill Jeremiah's prophecy of their continuance as long as this world lasts. How wonderful is God's knowledge and wisdom and how amazing was His plan to use His chosen but unbelieving nation through the centuries!

ISRAEL NOT CAST AWAY

We are ready now to turn to Romans 11:1 to hear Paul's

answer to this important question:

> I say then, Hath God cast away His people? God forbid.
> For I also am an Israelite of the seed of Abraham, of the
> tribe of Benjamin. God hath not cast away His people
> which he foreknew (Romans 11:1,2a).

Paul uses his own example, being an Israelite who was the
object of God's mercy now saved by Christ and a Christian, to
prove that Israel was not cast away. Salvation was still offered
to the people of Israel.

There are some who teach that the phrase in verse 2,
"...His people whom He foreknew" means that God saved the
believing remnant of Israel by election but did cast away the
physical nation as a whole. However, the saving of the
remnant was not only a proof that God had reserved for
Himself "an election," it was also the assurance of a future
day when the nation as a whole could be the object of His
mercy and grace. It was by saving the remnant during times
of apostasy and judgment when His wrath was poured out
upon the unbelieving and disobedient nation that made
possible the continued life of the nation when it was restored
and the judgment lifted.

So through the centuries God has been reserving a
remnant and sparing some of Israel for salvation, but now it
is evident that He plans to deal with them as a nation again
having driven many of the physical seed of Israel out from
the nations of the world back to Jerusalem and their homeland. Who can deny that there is a nation of the seed of
Abraham back in the land and that the Almighty Saviour can
manifest His grace toward Israel greater than all her sin by
removing the blindness He placed upon her and calling her
to salvation with His effectual calling? This is what is
promised in this great chapter in Romans.

PUNISHED BY BLINDNESS

It is clear that Paul in Romans chapter 11, makes a distinction between the believing remnant of Israel, or "the
election" (as he calls it), and the rest of national Israel who he
says "were blinded" (vs. 7). You may wonder what it means to
be "blinded." The apostle quotes from two Old Testament

39

passages to show that this blindness was according to the Scriptures:

> According as it is written, God hath given them the spirit of slumber, eyes that they should not see, and ears that they should not hear: unto this day. And David saith, Let their table be made a snare and a trap and a stumbling block and a recompence unto them: Let their eyes be darkened; that they may not see and bow down their back alway (Romans 11:8-10).

(See Psalms 69:22; Isaiah 6:10; also Mark 4:12.)

This spiritual blindness is a judgment which God places upon those who continually refuse to accept the light He tries to give and who stubbornly persist in disobedience. They see but they don't really perceive; they hear but they do not really understand. God was merciful in judging Israel only with a partial blindness. Had it been complete blindness on the nation totally, no Jews could have been saved. But Paul uses himself as an illustration that a Jew could be saved if he believes and recognizes that God has reserved a remnant for Himself during the period of national punishment.

Then he asks, "Have they stumbled that they should fall?" (vs. 11a). Here he unquestionably is talking about the nation as a whole that "was blinded" and has stumbled, not the believing remnant. And he tells us that through their fall "salvation is come unto the Gentiles, for to provoke them to jealousy" (vs. 11b). Moses, centuries before, had revealed that this would be God's method of dealing with His unbelieving nation. He had said in Deuteronomy 32:18, "Of the Rock that begat thee thou art unmindful, and hath forgotten God that formed thee," and Paul no doubt is quoting from this passage when he speaks of being "provoked to jealousy." Compare these words of Deuteronomy 32:21:

> They have moved me to jealousy with that which is not God: they have provoked me to anger with their vanities: and I will move them to jealousy with those which are not a people: I will provoke them to anger with a foolish nation.

It is important to remember that this promise was spoken

to the nation of Israel and that by using "a foolish nation" He would provoke Israel to jealousy. Paul might hope that by some means he might provoke "some" of his blinded nation to jealousy but this speaks of God using a foolish nation to provoke Israel which is quite different. Certainly, the apostle did not have much success in reaching the Jews in Rome (Acts 28:25-28), and Israel nationally still has not been provoked to jealousy and to return to God and faith in her Messiah. This is still to happen.

SOMETHING STILL AHEAD

In the 12th and 15th verses of Romans 11, we have a definite prophecy that there is something future for Israel. Since it is plain that Paul is talking not of the believing remnant but of the nation that stumbled, we look for a great blessing to come to that restored nation, which is now in the land of Israel. Notice how the apostle puts it: "Now if the fall of them (the unbelieving nation) be the riches of the world, and the diminishing of them the riches of the Gentiles: how much more their fullness?" (vs. 12) and "For if the casting away of them be the reconciling of the world, what shall the receiving of them be but life from the dead? (vs. 15). Just what kind of blessing this means for the Gentiles it is difficult to say. Some teach that the phrase "life from the dead" means resurrection and consequently connect it with the return of Jesus and The Resurrection Day. They read it to mean that when the full number of elect believers from among the Jews throughout the age of grace has been received, then the resurrection will take place. But this is a forced and unnatural interpretation of the Apostle's words. How much more reasonable and better to accept the plain meaning of what he says, i.e., the receiving of them (Israel) can be nothing but life from death (spiritual life from spiritual death). It is just what the Father says of the prodigal son in Jesus' parable when he returned home again. "For this my son was dead and is alive again; he was lost and is found. And they began to be merry" (Luke 15:24). When Israel was under God's judgment in captivity in Babylon, the prophet Ezekiel was given a vision of a valley filled with dry bones that were brought together by God's power and given new life. This gave promise of the rebirth of the nation of

Israel after 70 long years of national death and sorrow in a strange land which occurred in 536 B.C. How much greater will be the joy and wonder in the Father's house and in the church when after more than nineteen centuries of spiritual death with partial blindness upon the nation the day comes when Israel as a nation receives life from the dead.

Others suggest that with the "fullness" and the "receiving" of national Israel in verses 12 and 15, there will come a sweeping worldwide conversion of Gentiles with multitudes being saved through the witness of Jews who have come to believe in Jesus the Messiah. However, there are two reasons that make it impossible to find this teaching in these words of Paul. One, he definitely tells us that the riches came to the Gentiles through the *fall* of Israel and the world was reconciled by their *being cast away*, not by their "fullness" or "receiving." And two, in verse 25 of chapter 11 he tells us that the partial judgment of blindness will remain on Israel until "the full number of Gentiles be come in." If the full or complete number of Gentiles have already been gathered in before the eyes of Israel are opened, how can you have another great number of Gentiles converted after the blindness is removed? No, the real blessing that will come as a result of the "fullness" and "receiving" of Israel will be the experience of the marvelous riches of grace in Christ as the work of salvation is crowned with the spiritual resurrection of the nation chosen by God, the nation of our Lord's kinsmen according to the flesh bringing them back into the household of faith.

In this important 11th chapter of Romans, Paul uses the parable of the olive tree to express the vital relation of believers to the root, which is Christ, both Jewish branches, which are called "natural branches" and Gentile branches called "wild by nature." The trunk no doubt is Abraham, the father of the faithful, but the root must be the Lord Jesus, the promised Seed, from whom life really must come (John 15:1). Belief is the key to the vital union of the branch which is grafted into the trunk of the olive tree and Paul warns the Gentiles against being highminded because the natural branches, the Jews, were broken off through their unbelief. If they (the Jews) remain not in unbelief, they will be grafted in "for God is able to graft them in again" (Romans 11:23). No one is secure in Christ unless He truly believes and lives by faith, and Paul argues that if the wild olive branches (the

Gentiles) can be grafted into the olive tree, how much more can the natural branches, the Jews, be grafted back into their own olive tree, *if* they will believe.

Then in Romans 11:25, we have the revelation of a mystery which Dr. H.C.G. Moule in his *Commentary on the Epistle to the Romans* says is "one of the most definitely predictive of all the prophetic utterances of the Epistles." This, he says, is:

> its message on the whole; that there lies hidden in the future, for the race of Israel, a critical period of over-whelming blessing....We have heard the Apostle speak fully and without compromise, of the sin of Israel; the hardened or paralyzed spiritual perception, the refusal to submit to pure grace, the restless quest for a valid self-righteousness, the deep exclusion arrogance. And thus the promise of coming mercy, such as shall surprise the world, sounds all the more sovereign and magnificent.*

What is this mystery, now revealed? Let Paul say it:

> For I would not brethren that ye should be ignorant of this mystery, lest ye should be wise in your own conceits: that blindness in part is happened to Israel, until the fullness of the Gentiles be come in. And so all Israel shall be saved (Romans 11:25,26a).

GREAT DAY OF GRACE

Here we have the final fulfillment of God's promise to His people: the judgmental partial blindness placed upon Israel nationally 1900 years ago and kept there through these centuries will one day be taken away. A great multitude of Jews will see the Saviour with the eye of faith and believe, so many, in fact, that Paul can say, "And thus (so) all Israel shall be saved," corresponding to the "fullness" of Israel (verse 12), and the "receiving" of Israel as alive from the dead (verse 15). Remember, it will be only through individual personal faith that Israel will be saved for the Apostle said in

---

*H.C.G. Moule, *Commentary on the Epistle to the Romans*, p. 308.

verse 23, "And they also (the Jews) if they abide not still in unbelief shall be grafted in: for God is able to graft them in again."

ALL ISRAEL SAVED

What does the Apostle mean when he says in verse 26, "And so all Israel shall be saved"? First, Paul's quotation from Isaiah 59:20,21, definitely indicates that national Israel is meant for he says:

> ...as it is written, There shall come out of Zion, a Deliverer, and shall turn away ungodliness from Jacob; for this is my covenant unto them when I shall take away their sins.

The name, Jacob, is used collectively for the nation of Israel; the covenant is unto *them;* and He will take away *their* sins. Surely this must refer to the nation that has been reconstituted in the land of their forefathers, and now is in a position to receive the salvation of God as His people.

Second, the words "be saved" must be taken in the sense in which Paul is using them in this entire passage. He confessed to great sorrow and heaviness of heart because of his nation's unbelief and the wrath that was coming upon them. He describes them as having heard but as rejecting the gospel of righteousness by faith and pictures God as stretching out His arms to them "all day long" even though they were rebellious and unbelieving. And he specifically says my heart's desire is that they might be saved. What he means is made clear in Romans 10:9,10 "That if thou shalt confess with thy mouth the Lord Jesus and believe in thine heart that God has raised Him from the dead, thou shalt be saved." This salvation then must be the result of the removal of the partial blindness and of God's mercy and forgiveness that enables the people of Israel to see with spiritual understanding the awful sin of rejecting their Messiah, the only Saviour, who still offers His love to them and calls them by His Holy Spirit.

Third, the word "so" or "thus" has been wrongly thought by some to mean "then" ("and then all Israel shall be saved"). They hold that when the full number of Gentiles have come into the church, Jesus will return to rapture His bride, receiving her to Himself in the air. He doesn't come to earth but somehow He reveals Himself to Israel so they see Him with their physical eyes and are convinced by seeing Him that they should believe on Him. Thus, Israel is saved and by preaching the gospel of the Kingdom, they will win many to Christ from the Gentile nations and prepare for the millennial kingdom. Nowhere in Scripture are we taught that when the full number of Gentiles is gathered in, the church will be complete. In fact, the church is to be "one new man in Christ Jesus," composed of both Jew and Gentile. Having kept Israel nationally under judgment of spiritual partial blindness for nineteen centuries, there is every reason to believe that when the judgment is lifted, Israel will have her day of grace with the opportunity to be saved. Furthermore, it is contrary to God's plan of salvation to think that any person or group of people can be saved by seeing Jesus with just the physical eyesight. We live by faith, not by sight. The prophecy of Zechariah 12:10, "They shall look upon Me whom they pierced" is quoted in John 19:37 and said to be fulfilled when Jesus hung on the cross. Nowhere in the New Testament do we find any scripture teaching that the Jews will be saved by seeing Jesus. Certainly this passage in Romans 11 is teaching salvation for them on a national scale by faith when the spiritual blindness is removed and that will take place when the full number of Gentiles have been gathered into the body of believers.

Someone has suggested that in his opinion the notion is "completely unacceptable that after the entrance of the Gentiles into the glorified reality of God, there will still be time and place in the present dispensation for Israel to come to its senses and be converted," but who dares limit God to a time frame? The place is certainly available—Israel! And the time? How long will it take God to remove the blindness from the nation? Already they observe each year 'A Day of Atonement' preceded by days of confession of sin. With the judgment lifted and if God breathes His Spirit upon them, who will say that the nation could not have a spiritual rebirth in a day? The nation of Israel was guilty of helping to put Jesus on the cross but He prayed as He hung there between heaven and earth, "Father, forgive them for they know not what they do." How long would it take for this prayer to be answered if they turned and sought Him with all their heart?

But, is national Israel all that Paul means when he says, "And so all Israel shall be saved"? Didn't the apostle define the true Israel as the believing sons of Abraham? (Romans 9:6-8). The seed of faith, including both Jews and Gentiles, are the true children of Abraham, not the children who are only his physical descendants. And has not Paul just spoken of the "fullness" of the Gentiles" coming in, which means being grafted into the olive tree and thus being part of the household of faith? I believe that the phrase "all Israel shall be saved" means not only a great individual repentance and faith by many in national Israel, but also the completion of the entire household of faith including the "fullness of the Gentiles" who are saved.

This is borne out as the apostle continues with this tremendous thought in Romans 11. In verse 28, he recognizes that "as concerning the gospel, they (the Jews) are enemies for your sakes" for they were persecuting the Christians and opposing the preaching of the Gospel of Christ wherever possible. But "as touching the election, they are beloved for the fathers' sakes," i.e., because they are the children of Abraham, Isaac and Jacob. "For the gifts and calling of God are without repentance" (verse 29). God is faithful to His promise to Abraham and His Seed and when He promised "to turn away ungodliness from Jacob," He will do it.

SPIRITUAL RENEWAL

Notice that this is a promise, not of material blessing or of the restoration of Israel to worldly power. Rather it is a promise of spiritual renewal, of righteousness and cleansing which mean salvation and eternal blessedness with the Father.

Notice, too, that nothing is said here of seeing Jesus when He returns, but rather the promise is made of the removal of spiritual blindness so Israel can see with the eye of faith. And if they believe, they will want to be baptized into the name of the Father, and of the Son, and of the Holy Ghost, and enter into fellowship with the members of the church, the Bride of Christ. It will be a glorious time, like the days of the apostles when "the Lord added to His church daily such as should be saved" (Acts 2:47b).

In Romans 11:32 and 33, Paul emphasizes again the wonderful interrelation in the plan of salvation between Jew and Gentile.

> For as ye (Gentiles) in times past have not believed God, yet have now obtained mercy through their unbelief: Even so have these also now not believed, that through your mercy they also may obtain mercy. For God hath concluded them all in unbelief, that He might have mercy upon all.

What a plan of saving a lost world through a Saviour-King, having proven that righteousness could not be obtained through the works of the flesh by keeping the law. Only through faith in One who is the Lamb of God that taketh away the sin of the world and by submitting to the Lordship of Him whose right it is to sit upon the Throne can anyone be saved. God leveled all of humanity so there was no advantage of birth, of position, of wealth, of power, of race, or of nation. He concluded all under unbelief, the only sin that if persisted in cannot be forgiven, that He might have mercy upon all alike, Jew and Gentile, and open the door to all who will believe.

In some manuscripts of the Scripture, there is a third "now" used in this verse so that it would read:

> Even so have these also now not believed, that through your mercy they also may now obtain mercy.

This means, it is said by some, that the interplay of Jew and Gentile first in bringing Gentile salvation by the unbelief of the Jews was already at work bringing Jewish salvation through Gentile mercy. It would refer then to the elect remnant who were being saved among the Jews as the gospel was preached to them. But Paul cannot mean this by what he is saying. He has just said that the unbelief of the Jews involved in the judgment of blindness upon them would continue until the full number of Gentiles were gathered in which obviously had not happened at that time. He is talking of something that was to happen in the future, an unknown future but a definite point of time when on a national scale salvation, the deliverance from sin, would come to Israel. Remember Paul's use of the word "now" in II Corinthians 6:2, "now is the accepted time; now is the day of salvation" which means the present age of gospel preaching. Before this day of opportunity closes, while it is still the accepted time, we believe that Israel nationally will be saved.

DOXOLOGY

As the apostle thinks of these truths, all he can do is bow his heart in reverent adoration. And we do well if we join him in true and humble worship acknowledging in his words:

The depth of the riches both of the wisdom and knowledge of God! How unsearchable are His judgments and His ways past finding out!

He is a God of infinite love and mercy whose grace is greater than all our sin. And when the fullness of the Gentiles is come in to the church which started in the days following the resurrection of our Lord as a church of Jews who believed in Jesus as their Messiah, God will close this age with a final display of His saving grace to a rebellious nation held under judgment for 19 centuries and Israel shall be saved. The world of Christians will rejoice at the witness of Israel made alive unto Christ by the power of His resurrection, testifying before the nations that He is Lord to the glory of God the Father. Can there be any greater expectation for Israel than a day of grace when the partial blindness is removed and all who will believe will be saved and inherit the blessings of salvation which believers of all generations have found through faith in Christ, the Messiah? Can there be any greater hope for Israel than to complete the Bride of Christ, to be grafted back into their own olive tree and to be part of the Kingdom of God's dear Son? His is not an earthly millennial kingdom in which death still takes its toll and which will be climaxed when Satan makes a final but futile rebellion through God and Magog (Rev. 20:7,8), but it is an everlasting, heavenly kingdom, which includes the redeemed of all generations and from every nation and will continue forever.*

---

*See Appendix B on the interpretation of Revelation 20:1-9.

ISRAEL IN THE LAND

It is important that we understand why God has brought Israel back into the land. With the exception of the 70-year period of captivity from 606-536 B.C., God preserved His chosen people in the land for more than twelve centuries, to give witness to the rest of the world to His commandments, His providence, His justice and His mercy. This witness was at last given in perfection when Jesus, born of the seed of Abraham and of David, came and in that land revealed the Father's love, His judgment upon sin, His everlasting righteousness, His forgiving grace and His mighty power over death and the kingdom of Satan. It was from that land that the new commandment of love went forth to the ends of the earth and it is to that land, where on a hill called Calvary, the Son of God was nailed to a cruel cross, that the eyes of all people in the world are invited to look for salvation. And it was from that land that humble ambassadors of Christ went forth into a hostile world preaching the kingdom of God and claiming every continent and even the farthest isles of the sea as the inheritance of their Lord, the King of Kings and Lord of Lords. Was the land important to God in His plan of redemption as He carried it out in history? Certainly it was! Abraham sojourned in that land led by the God who promised him a Seed that would bless the nations of the earth. The tribes of Israel conquered the land and divided it as their inheritance according to God's promise to Abraham, Isaac and Jacob. Solomon in all his glory ruled the land in the zenith of Israel's national life and became the wonder of the nations. But a greater than Solomon came to that land of Israel to save the world from sin and by His death upon the cross and His resurrection from the grave, His Name is revered and worshipped by millions and known in every nation. Yes, the land was important to God in His redemptive plan.

But why should Israel be back in the land today, after centuries of exile, and why would God allow them to come back as a nation, still rejecting His Son, their Messiah? Do you realize that if the Jews had all accepted Jesus as their Messiah, they would have become part of the church, the Body and the Bride of Christ? This was God's expressed desire as the Scripture says, "That He might make in Himself of twain (Jew and Gentile) one new man in Christ"

(Ephesians 2:15b). For the Christian, whether of Jewish or Gentile background, there is no need for the homeland in Palestine; he has become heir of a city having foundations whose builder and maker is God. But generation after generation of Jews since 70 A.D. have for the most part remained in unbelief and consequently under judicial blindness but have longed to be back in the land.

The return then of Israel to the homeland in unbelief must have been accomplished for two reasons: (1) to fulfill the prophecy made by Jesus that "Jerusalem shall be trodden down of the Gentiles until the times of the Gentiles be fulfilled," implying Jewish control to follow; (2) in order to fulfill Paul's revelation of the mystery that the blindness on Israel would be removed when the fullness of the Gentiles is come in (Romans 11:25), and Israel nationally would be received upon the condition of faith and grafted in again with the Gentiles into the same olive tree. Evidently in God's program it is necessary for them to be back in the land as a nation when the judgment of blindness is removed and when He calls them as a nation to repentance and faith in His Son, the Messiah. Abba Eban writes in the beautifully illustrated book, *Promised Land*, that one thing is clear:

> It is in Israel alone that the Jew can face the world in its own authentic image and not as a footnote in the story of other societies. It is only as a nation in its own soil, its own tongue, and its own faith that the Jewish people can hear what it has to hear, say what it has to say, do what it has to do.*

How prophetic are these words! How wonderfully God is preparing the people in the Land for the day when He removes the blindness from their eyes and they will bear witness before the world of His amazing grace and undying love. Remember, the church will still be in the world to welcome them into the fellowship of God's people and to rejoice in an Israel redeemed by the blood of the Lamb of God. Note that I refuse to call the church a Gentile church; for I believe it is Christ's church in which

---

*Abba Eban, *Promised Land*, p. 152.

there is neither Jew nor Greek, there is neither bond nor free, there is neither male nor female; for ye are all one in Christ Jesus. And if ye be Christ's, then are ye Abraham's seed and heirs according to the promise (Galatians 3:28,29).

Note, also that I insist that this must take place before the rapture of the church, otherwise Paul's metaphor of believing Israel being "grafted in again" becomes meaningless should there be no church left on earth into which it could be grafted (Romans 11:23,24).

STAGE IS SET

God has set the stage for the climax of human history. These are tremendous days in which this generation is living. We believe that the coming of our Lord Jesus is near at hand. The Gospel is being preached around the world and is passing through all barriers and reaching into every nation by radio. Israel has been a nation in the land for nearly forty years. Worldwide apostasy by many from the truth of God's Word is very evident. Deterioration of moral standards, the rise of crime and violence, the spread of humanism, materialism, atheism, and false cults—these conditions surely make one feel Satan has been let loose and that the Anti-Christ, the man of sin, may appear on the world stage at any time. The unbelieving people of the world will be in a condition of moral rebellion against God like the days of Noah and of the wicked cities of Sodom and Gomorrah. Having brought into the church the full number of Gentiles, God will send a strong delusion upon the unbelieving people of the world that they may believe a lie (II Thessalonians 2:11). At the same time, He will remove the judgment of spiritual blindness from the nation of Israel and will call many, perhaps most, of her people to repentance and faith in the Messiah, the Lord Jesus. This will be the crowning act of His saving and redeeming mercy, completing the "one new man" in Christ, perfecting the Bride and putting the capstone upon the living temple which He has been building through the centuries.

If we are right in believing that the conversion of Israel nationally, with the judgmental blindness removed, will take place before the rapture and will complete God's purpose of calling out of the world the church composed of Jewish and Gentile believers made one in Christ, then surely we must be praying for this to happen and expecting that it will occur at any time.

I can see a very close parallel between the situation of the Jews in the captivity in Babylon 25 centuries ago and the present situation of Israel today. Daniel had read in Jeremiah's prophecy that Israel would be kept in captivity for seventy years and then God would return them to the land. In Romans 11, we read not of a return to the land, but of a return to God when the fullness of the Gentiles is come in and the partial blindness is removed from the scattered nation. Just as Daniel turned to the Lord in prayer on behalf of his people, so today we Christians should turn to God beseeching Him to pour His grace and mercy upon the nation "beloved for the fathers' sake" that they might return from a captivity of bondage to a hardened and rebellious spiritual condition and, through their Messiah, be brought by repentance and faith into the liberty and freedom of the sons of God. This burden of prayer should be on every believer who desires to see the family of God complete and ready for the coming of our glorious Saviour.

We not only should pray for Israel to be converted to faith in Jesus but also confess the failure of the church in its attitude toward the Jews through the centuries. Dr. Moule in his *Commentary on the Epistle to the Romans* points out the

responsibility upon the church of Christ, not only for the flagrant wrong of having too often animated and directed the civil power in its oppression of Israel, and not only for having so awfully neglected to seek the evangelization of Israel by direct appeals for the true messiah, and by an open setting forth of His glory, but for the deeper and more subtle wrong, persistently inflicted from age to age, in a most guilty unconsciousness—the wrong of having failed to manifest Christ to

Israel through the living holiness of Christendom.*

Through the fall of the Jews, salvation came to the Gentiles "for to provoke Israel to jealousy" (compare Deuteronomy 32:21), but the Christian church as a whole has not shown much sincere love for the Jewish people nor has it given the kind of testimony that would draw them to Jesus because they could see the purity, the peace, the joy and the glorious hope in the lives of His followers. Even now there is little evidence of a sincere desire to see Jews converted and welcomed in Christ's love into the midst of the churches that profess the Saviour's Name. How different it would be if we really felt the burden to pray for God's mercy on Israel and if we extended from our hearts a warm, earnest invitation to come to their Messiah, backed up with the testimony of a pure, selfless, love-filled life. This is the burden that compelled me to write this book. God is faithful who will fulfill His promise to Israel—the promise contained in the mystery revealed by Paul in Romans 11:25. The blindness on Israel will continue only until the fullness of the Gentiles are come in and then the fullness of the Jews will be grafted back in, their receiving as a nation that has been so long under judgment will be as "life from the dead" (Romans 11:12,15).

Will you accept this burden for Israel and urge others to join with you in sharing it? Will you help to prepare the church as well as Israel for this wonderful climax of God's redemptive plan?

---

*H.C.G. Moule, *Commentary on the Epistle to the Romans*, p. 296.

Part II

GOD'S COVENANTAL RELATIONSHIP WITH ISRAEL

CHAPTER IV

Israel's Covenant Through Abraham

THE COVENANT WHICH GOD MADE with Abraham is of supreme importance in our study of God's purpose with Israel. All Christian Bible expositors are agreed that this forms the foundation of God's dealings with the nation of Israel and also gave promise to the redemptive work of Jesus Christ. But there are such varying opinions as to the implications of the covenant and the interpretation of its meaning to Israel and the Church that we must consider this step in God's unfolding program of redemption most carefully lest we follow a misconceived false view and end in total disagreement with the New Testament.

That the Abrahamic covenant is a step in the revelation of God's plan of redemption is very clear as we look back to the earlier chapters in Genesis. There, according to the familiar story, God placed Adam and Eve in the Garden of Eden and, having surrounded them with the blessings of His handiwork, tested their obedience to His will. When they sinned by disobeying their Creator, God pronounced judgment upon them but gave them hope of deliverance through the seed of the woman (Genesis 3:15). Messiah would crush the head of the serpent, though in the conflict He Himself would bruise His heel. Adam lived through nine centuries but no redeemer came. The world grew steadily worse until man's mind and heart were so corrupt that God destroyed the earth with a flood, saving only eight souls, Noah and his family. Later God again came down with judgment upon the people who tried to reach heaven by building the tower of Babel and he scattered them by confounding their languages. Finally, God was ready to prepare for the coming of the Redeemer of Mankind and He chose Abraham to be the one through whom the promised Seed should come.

PROMISES TO ABRAHAM

Following are sixteen promises given to Abraham by the Almighty God as He confirmed the covenant with him and his Seed. We shall find that some of these were made with respect to his physical seed or descendants but that the primary unconditional promises of blessing to all nations and of possessing the gate of his enemies were made with respect to the Seed, the Messiah and in Him to the seed of faith. Here then are the promises:

1. Genesis 12:2   I will make of thee a great nation.

2. Genesis 12:2   I will bless thee.

3. Genesis 12:2   I will make thy name great.

4. Genesis 12:2   Thou shalt be a blessing.

5. Genesis 12:3   I will bless them that bless thee.

6. Genesis 12:3   And curse him that curseth thee.

7. Genesis 12:3   In thee shall all families of the earth be blessed.

8. Genesis 12:7   Unto thy seed I will give this land.

9. Genesis 13:15   All the land which thou seest, to thee will I give it and to thy seed forever.

10. Genesis 13:16   I will make thy seed as the dust of the earth.

11. Genesis 17:4   Thou shalt be a father of many nations.

12. Genesis 17:6   I will make nations of thee.

13. Genesis 17:6   Kings shall come out of thee.

14. Genesis 17:7   I will establish my covenant between me and thee.

15. Genesis 22:17   Thy seed shall possess the gate of his enemies.

16. Genesis 22:18   And in thy Seed shall all the nations of the earth be blessed; because thou hast obeyed my voice.

The importance of the promise to Abraham is underscored in Hebrews 6:13-20 where the writer says,

> For when God made promise to Abraham, because He could swear by no greater He swore by Himself, saying, 'Surely blessing I will bless thee, and multiplying I will multiply thee.' And so, after he had patiently endured, he obtained the promise....Wherein God willing more abundantly to shew unto the heirs of promise the immutability of His counsel confirmed it by an oath: that by two immutable things in which it was impossible for God to lie, we might have a strong consolation, who have fled for refuge to lay hold upon the hope set before us: which hope we have as an anchor of the soul, both sure and steadfast and which entereth into that within the veil; whither the forerunner is for us entered even Jesus, made an high priest forever after the order of Melchizedek.

God even sealed His Word of promise to Abraham with an oath and the glorious result is our absolute confidence in the eternal hope set before all believers, both Jews and Gentiles, who are in Christ.

SALVATION THROUGH CHRIST

God was and is primarily interested in the salvation of the soul and to that end He purposed to bring the blessing of the Gospel to all men everywhere. Other things such as the promise of the land, material blessing, possession of the land, the kings that should come out of Abraham, and the ritual feasts—these are less important and subservient to His great promise to bless all the nations on earth through the Seed, Jesus Christ.

When Peter preached to the Jews on the day of Pentecost, he said,

> Repent, and be baptized everyone of you in the name of Jesus Christ for the remission of sins, and ye shall receive the gift of the Holy Ghost. For the promise is unto you and to your children, and to all that are afar off, even as many as the Lord our God shall call (Acts 2:38,39).

What "promise" is Peter referring to? Certainly to the promise that was Israel's hope given to Abraham to be fulfilled by the Messiah. In another New Testament passage the writer of Hebrews, after recalling the heroes of faith, says,

> And these all having obtained a good report through faith, received not the promise: God having provided some better thing for us [Christians] that they without us should not be made perfect (Hebrews 11:39,40).

Again, we have the promise which Israel's spiritual heroes longed to see fulfilled, withheld from them so that the promise might include all for whom God intended it, including all believers in the church.

When Paul preached in the synagogue in Pisidian Antioch to an audience of Jews and some Gentiles, he said,

> And we declare unto you glad tidings, how that the promise which was made unto the fathers, God hath fulfilled the same unto us their children, in that He hath raised up Jesus again: as it is also written in the second Psalm, Thou art my Son, this day have I begotten Thee (Acts 13:32,33).

Here Paul distinctly and clearly says that God had fulfilled His promise made to the fathers in Jesus Christ and especially in His resurrection.

These passages are sufficient to emphasize the truth that

God was primarily interested in providing forgiveness of sins through Abraham's Seed for both Israel and the Gentiles and that this is the heart of the covenant promise. According to St. Paul, writing in Galatians chapter 3, the promise was not made to the seed of Abraham, *plural*, referring to the physical descendants but it was made "to Abraham and his Seed" in the *singular*, telling us that it was to Christ and all who are in Him (Galatians 3:16). Let us keep this in mind as we study the promises to Abraham and try to understand all that is included.

PROGRESSIVE REVELATION

The Covenant of Promise was not given in its entirety to Abraham at one point in his life but in a series of appearances of God to this great man whom God chose to be His friend. There is progressive revelation of God's purpose and will during a period of at least forty years with appearances of God to Abraham, recorded in Genesis 12:1-3,7; 13:14-17; 15:1-21; 17:1-22; 21:12,13; 22:15-18. Let us consider carefully the following great moments when God met Abraham during this period.

A. Genesis 12:1-3,7

At the age of 75, Abram was told to leave his country, his kindred, and his father's house and go to a land that God would show him and God promised

> I will make of thee a great nation, and I will bless thee and make thy name great; and thou shalt be a blessing; and I will bless them that bless thee and curse him that curseth thee: and in thee shall all the families of the earth be blessed (Genesis 12:2-3).

Most of God's promise here is to Abraham personally— a great nation would come of him (even though he is childless) and world-wide blessing would come through him. The first mention of the land is in verse 7 when he had arrived in Canaan and God simply says, "Unto thy seed will I give this land."

B. Genesis 13:14-17

Several years passed and after the quarrel between Lot and Abraham when Lot chose to go into the area of Sodom, as recorded in Genesis 13, God again came to Abram. This time God specifies that He will give to Abram's seed all the land he can see to the north, south, east, and west and would give it to the seed forever. (Since we are talking of material land, which cannot be permanent, we recognize that the meaning of "forever" is not to be understood in the sense of ever-lasting or eternal but "perpetually.") And God also promised that his seed would be as the dust of the earth, no doubt referring to his physical seed (although at this time Abraham had no son).

C. Genesis 15:1-21

Some time later after Abram rescued Lot from the five kings who had captured Sodom, God came to him and said, "Fear not, Abram; I am thy shield and thy exceeding great reward" (Genesis 15:1). Then when Abram reminded God that he had no seed to be his heir, God revealed that the steward of his house should not inherit his possessions but "he that shall come forth out of thine own bowels shall be thine heir" (Genesis 15:4). In connection with this God renews the promise of Abram's numberless seed and at this point God's Word records that Abram "believed in the Lord and He counted it to him for righteousness." St. Paul quotes these words and makes the supremely important point that Abraham's faith came before he was in circumcision in order "that he might be the father of them that believe, though they be not circumcised, that righteousness might be imputed unto them also" (Romans 4:11b). Paul also declares that "the promise that he should be the heir of the world was not to Abraham or to his seed through the law but through the righteousness of faith" (Romans 4:13). This is crucially important to remember for it is plain that the promise was given through the believing seed of Abraham (ultimately the Seed which is Christ) but through the history of the nation of Israel it was always the believing seed that fulfilled God's purpose, those "who are not only of the circumcision but who also walk in the steps of that faith of our father

Abraham" (Romans 4:12).

As we ponder these words given to Paul by the inspiration of the Holy Spirit, we can see the supreme importance of faith in our relation to God. "Without faith it is impossible to please God." This is not only true of the individual but also of Israel as a nation. God kept Israel under the law until the Promised Seed (the Messiah) came, but it was when Israel's leaders truly believed and acted in faith that God's blessing was poured out upon the nation. Unbelieving Israel had no special claim upon the mercy of God but when there was true repentance and obedience in faith, then God was always quick to respond with blessing. We must remember this as we continue to study the covenant and promise God made with Abraham and His Seed.

LAND PROMISED

Having told Abram that he, though an old man, would truly have his own seed, God proceeded with the revelation of the period of bondage in Egypt when his seed would be sorely afflicted and after the fourth generation they would return to the land. On that same day the Lord made a covenant with Abram saying, "Unto thy seed have I given this land from the river of Egypt unto the great river Euphrates" (Genesis 15:18). Notice that God does not say in verse 18 that this gift of land will be forever as He does of the land of Canaan in Genesis 13:15 and 17:8. Some claim that the promise of the larger area from Egypt to the Euphrates has never been fulfilled and we must expect a future fulfillment. But nothing could be plainer than the Scripture itself in I Kings 4:21,24 where we read,

> And Solomon reigned over all kingdoms from the river to the land of the Philistines and unto the border of Egypt: they brought presents and served Solomon all the days of his life....For he had dominion over all the region on this side of the river from Tiphsah even to Azzah, over all the kings on this side the river: and he had peace on all sides round about him.

Some argue that Israel did not really possess all of this territory but surely David and Solomon believed that it had been conquered and was subject to them for over forty years and the clear statement in Scripture is enough for me to believe that God fulfilled His Word to Abraham.

Also the land of Canaan, which was promised to Abraham's seed, was fully given to them and they possessed it. Moses gives a detailed description of the areas to be divided among the twelve tribes as their inheritance (Numbers 34:1-15). Then near the close of the life of Joshua who led the conquest of Canaan we read in Joshua 21:43,45,

> And the Lord gave unto Israel all the land which He swore to give unto their fathers: and they possessed it and dwelt therein....There failed not ought of any good thing which the Lord had spoken unto Israel: all came to pass.

Even before their entrance into the land of promise Moses warned the nation that if they were disobedient and failed to love God they would be destroyed from off the land (Deuteronomy 4:25,26). But he also promised that if from their dispersion they would seek the Lord their God they would find him if they "seek Him with all their heart and with all their soul" (Deuteronomy 4:29). Joshua likewise warns Israel and declares that their continuance in the land is conditioned on obedience and faithfulness to God's commandments (Joshua 23:11-16). Notice how in Daniel's great prayer of confession before he received the revelation of the seventy weeks of years that were determined upon his people he definitely relates the Babylonian captivity as the great evil prophesied by Moses in the law because of their sin (Daniel 9:11-14).

UNCONDITIONAL PROMISE?

Is the promise of the land still in force and was it given to Israel unconditionally without respect to Israel's faithfulness or obedience? Is the present occupation of the land the result of Israel's obedience and her seeking the Lord with all her heart and with all her soul or is it occupied because Jews found it too dangerous to live as a separate people scattered among nations that so often were hostile to them? Certainly Israel today is a nation that does not believe in Jesus the

Messiah who came to redeem her. She has allowed atheists to be citizens but has refused to accept a Jew who believes that Jesus is the Messiah. She penalizes any who change their faith and become believers and she seeks to repress any Christian evangelism in her land. It is evident that Israel returned to the land in unbelief, not as a nation humbly seeking God's forgiveness of her sins and filled with faith and obedience to the Holy Scriptures. She has fought four wars to gain possession of and maintain herself in her homeland. Obviously this has all been in the plan of the Sovereign God. If the Jews had sought the Lord with all their heart and found Jesus to be their Messiah, they would have become Christians, a part of the Body of Christ, His Church, and there would have been no need for an earthly homeland. But our Lord had prophesied that "Jerusalem would be trodden down of the Gentiles until the times of the Gentiles be fulfilled" (Luke 21:24) and it was necessary that the nation, which has been under God's judgmental blindness for nineteen centuries, should come into possession of the Beloved City once again. In these final decades He "drove them out of the nations where they had settled" in order to fulfill His Word and has given them control of Jerusalem.

What purpose did God have in giving a land to the seed of Abraham? Was it not that His people might live in a land cleansed from idolatry and the abominations of the nations, separate from all other people, a testimony and witness of a people living under the law of God and therefore enjoying the blessings of His mercy and love? What a tragic story of failure is revealed in the parable of the wicked husbandmen told by Jesus near the final days of His earthly ministry (Matthew 21:33-45). Israel was the vineyard of God's planting which God nurtured, cultivated and prepared and then let it out to husbandmen. When God sent prophets to secure fruit from the vineyard, they were beaten, stoned and some killed. At last the Son was sent and sought the owner's fruit that was due but they killed Him. Plainly Jesus is reviewing the rebellion and sin of the nation of Israel which culminated in the cry, "Crucify Him." After the complete failure of the Old Covenant given by Moses and after the New Covenant was confirmed by the sacrifice of God's Son, then the middle wall of partition was broken down, Jew and Gentile were made one in the body of Christ and believers were scattered among all nations to be a witness to the gospel of salvation. Surely there was no need for a testimony of a people in the land and consequently, God uprooted the chosen nation from their homeland and the land had no significance in their history until He was ready to fulfill Jesus' prophecy of Israel's future restoration to the land and the control of Jerusalem.

Why did God bring Israel back to the land then? Was it that He wants to rebuild the wall between Jew and Gentile which Jesus broke down by the blood of His Cross? Was it that He might restore Israel to the Old Mosaic Covenant that made Israel a nation distinct from all other nations, with the temple rebuilt, a priesthood and sacrifices, feasts and other obligations? Certainly this is completely contrary to the entire teaching of the New Testament concerning our Lord's finished work of salvation which has made the Gentile believers "fellow citizens with the saints and of the household of God." It is far more reasonable to believe that God brought Israel back to the land in order that He might have the nation restored and He could remove the judgmental blindness from their eyes as a final testimony of His grace and mercy. What a witness to the world it will be when with the blindness removed they will see with spiritual sight the love and beauty and sacrifice of their Messiah and, as Paul says in Romans 11:23, "They also, if they abide not in unbelief, shall be grafted in: for God is able to graft them in again."

D. Genesis 17:1-22

A further strengthening of the Covenant Promise was given by God to Abram when he was 99 years old. Fourteen years before, Sarah and Abram, impatient that the promise of his own seed was not yet fulfilled, took the matter in their own hands and agreed that Abram should have a child by Sarah's handmaid. The child was born and was named Ishmael. Now he was thirteen years old when God appeared again to Abram and renewed the Covenant Promises. However, we note that in this passage He is definitely speaking to Abram concerning his seed according to the flesh, the natural descendants of this man who had not waited in faith for God to provide him a seed but had a child by a bond woman. There is no reference to the blessing that Abram would bring to all the nations of earth in the promises given at this time and note that this covenant was to be kept by the rite of circumcision throughout their generations on the part of Abraham and his **seed.** How amazing to see the way in which God unfolds **the covenant** relationship with both the physical and the **spiritual seed** of this great man chosen 4000 years ago! The covenant with the seed on the basis of the flesh is conditional as given in verses 1 and 2 of Genesis 17. "I am the Almighty God; walk before me and be thou perfect: and I will make my covenant between me and thee and will multiply thee exceedingly." Ishmael, Abram's son, was now thirteen and though rejected from the true Covenant of Promise, he would be fruitful and multiply exceedingly: "twelve princes shall he beget and I will make him a great nation" (Genesis 17:20) and he was included in the rite of circumcision which was binding on all of Abraham's seed.

CHILD OF FAITH

It is at this time that God promises that Sarah will bear Abraham a son and the covenant will be established with him, who was a child born of faith in the power of Almighty God. Isaac, even though a child of faith, was still a child of the flesh so we see in him the illustration of the true seed of Abraham, those who were not only natural descendants but who also walked in the way of Abraham's faith in God. Unless we keep this distinction in mind we will surely misunderstand God's program for the nation of Israel and fail to interpret aright the prophetic message of the Old Testament prophets as they foretold the coming of the Messiah. Ishmael was truly a son of Abraham, being a child of his flesh, born of a bond woman, but he was rejected because he was not the child of faith, born of the free woman. Read Galatians 4:22-31:

> For it is written, that Abraham had two sons: the one by a bondmaid, the other by a freewoman. But he who was of the bondwoman was born after the flesh; but he of the freewoman was by promise. Which things are an allegory; for these are the two covenants; the one from

the Mount Sinai, which gendereth to bondage, which is Agar. For this Agar is Mount Sinai in Arabia, and answereth to Jerusalem which now is, and is in bondage with her children. But Jerusalem which is above is free, which is the mother of us all. For it is written, Rejoice, thou barren that bearest not; break forth and cry, thou that travailest not; for the desolate hath many more children than she which hath an husband. Now we, brethren, as Isaac was, are the children of promise. But as then he that was born after the flesh, persecuted him that was born after the Spirit, even so it is now. Nevertheless what saith the scripture? Cast out the bondwoman and her son: for the son of the bondwoman shall not be heir with the son of the free-woman. So then, brethren, we are not children of the bondwoman, but of the free.

Paul uses this as an allegory and applies it to the relationship between Jews who would not believe in Jesus and all Christians. Ishmael, son of the bondwoman, stands for the Mosaic Covenant which held Jerusalem and her children in bondage to the law. But the heavenly Jerusalem is free whose children we Christians all are and "we brethren," Paul says, "as Isaac was, are the children of promise." Now he continues that just as Ishmael persecuted Isaac, so it was at that time the physical seed persecuted the spiritual seed. Quoting the Scripture, he says, "Cast out the bondwoman and her son: for the son of the bondwoman shall not be heir with the son of the freewoman" (Galatians 4:30). It is plain from this that Jews who are Abraham's children only by natural physical descent and not by having the same faith in the God of Abraham, are not reckoned as Abraham's true seed. God was very careful in making this unmistakably clear when He gave the Covenant Promise through Isaac and specifically rejected Ishmael (see also Romans 4:9-16 and 9:6-8).

E. Genesis 21:12,13

In this chapter we learn that at last God gave Abraham the seed of promise, the son of Sarah (the freewoman in contrast to the bondwoman) and Isaac was born when his father was one hundred years old. We do not need to spend much time here for we have already dealt with the rejection of Ishmael and the choice of Isaac as the son through whom the promised Seed was to come. The rejection of Ishmael certainly did not mean that God consigned all the seed of Ishmael to damnation and chose all the seed of Isaac to salvation. God in mercy met Hagar when she was banished from Sarah's presence and she exclaimed in surprise, "Thou God seest me!" (Genesis 16:13). God has always kept the door of faith open for any who truly seek after Him with all the heart but the enmity between the two sons of Abraham and between their seed has been a reminder of the continual conflict between the natural man and the spiritual man. Only as Israel was a believing people or nation has she represented the spiritual man.

F. Genesis 22:15-18

This is the climax of the Covenant Promise and it comes after Abraham had been given the ultimate test of faith and was proved faithful. God said to him,

> Take now thy son, thine only son Isaac, whom thou lovest and get thee into the land of Moriah: and offer him there for a burnt offering upon one of the mountains which I will tell thee of (Genesis 22:2).

What a test! He was asked to sacrifice to God his son Isaac, the only seed through whom the promise of blessing for the world was given. Was this contradicting all that God had been promising him? Was the covenant disavowed? What possible alternative was open to God to fulfill His Word if Isaac did not live? There was none so Abraham's faith took the ultimate step and he believed "that God was able to raise him up, even from the dead" (Hebrews 11:19). So God responded to the absolute faith of this great soul who actually placed the son of promise on the altar and was ready to plunge the knife into the heart of his own beloved child. He stopped the sacrifice saying,

> Lay not thine hand upon the lad neither do thou anything to him: for now I know that thou fearest God,

seeing thou hast not withheld thy son, thine only son from me.

How quickly and how easily our mind is transferred to the scene that took place on that same hill two thousand years later when God did not withhold His only Begotten Son but offered Him up for us all. Abraham's offering of his only son could not accomplish anything towards his redemption or eternal hope. It was simply the evidence that his heart was totally and absolutely committed in loving trust and obedience to the God who had led him for the past thirty-five years. In contrast, the offering of God's beloved Son on Calvary was an atoning sacrifice for the sin of the world for Jesus was the true Lamb of God.

When we analyze the words of the Apostle Paul in Galatians 3:27 we find a beautiful revelation of God's truth. He says,

> And this I say, that the covenant, that was confirmed before of God in Christ, the law which was four hundred and thirty years after cannot disannul, that it should make the promise of none effect.

Notice he does *not* say the covenant that has now been confirmed in Christ but "that was confirmed before of God in Christ"—confirmed before the law. There is no doubt in my mind that when Jesus said, "Abraham rejoiced to see my day and saw it and was glad" (John 8:56), He was referring to this experience on Mount Moriah when Abraham saw the substitute offering in the thicket and realized that God was teaching him the hope of the resurrection. For indeed the Scripture (Hebrews 11:19) says that he received Isaac back from the dead in a figure or figuratively speaking. No wonder St. Paul says that "the scripture, foreseeing that God would justify the heathen through faith, preached before the gospel unto Abraham" (Galatians 3:8).

This then is the moment when God reaffirmed the covenant with an oath and confirmed the promise in Christ, the true Seed. Though, of course, in this passage God does declare that the seed will be multiplied, the two great promises confirmed with an oath refer not to the seed of Israel as a nation but to the Seed of Abraham which is Christ. Which seed "shall possess the gate of his enemies"?

The nation or Christ? Let Scripture give the answer, "For He [Christ] must reign, till He hath put all enemies under His feet. The last enemy that shall be destroyed is death" (I Corinthians 15:25,26), and the promise to God's Son, "Ask of Me and I will give thee the heathen for thine inheritance and the uttermost part of the earth for thy possession (Psalm 2:8). In which seed were all the nations of the earth to be blessed? The physical seed, the nation or the true Seed which is Christ? Again the answer must be Christ for He Himself is the true vine (John 15:1) and He is the Saviour, the Lamb of God that taketh away the sin of the world.

> For God so loved the world that He gave His Only-begotten Son that whosoever believeth in Him should not perish but have everlasting life (John 3:16).

No, not the nation of Israel, but He who was the true Seed of Israel, the virgin-born Son of God, the Saviour of the world— He is All in All.

CHAPTER V

Israel's Covenant Through Moses

WHAT WAS THE PURPOSE of God in bringing Israel as a nation into the covenant relationship with Him? Was it not sufficient that He had made covenants and promises with Abraham, Isaac and Jacob? Why was it necessary to give them a system of laws and ritual sacrifices, feasts and observances with severe penalties if the laws were broken and promised blessings if they were obeyed? This we will attempt to consider in our present chapter.

The giving of the law through Moses was the event that truly constituted the nation as God's chosen people. God had forged the nation out of the descendants of the family of Jacob (Israel) in the crucible of suffering through years of affliction in Egyptian slavery. After He had delivered them with a mighty hand and led them to Mount Sinai in the wilderness, the Almighty called them to obedience to His revealed will. But St. Paul tells us that the law is the "ministration of death" for the law cannot save — it can only reveal and condemn sin (II Corinthians 3:6-9). So God also gave the nation a priesthood, a sacrifice, a Day of Atonement, and required of the people repentance and faith. Eventually He abrogated the Old Mosaic Covenant and made a New Covenant with Israel, sealed with the blood of His Son when Jesus offered Himself as the Lamb of God that taketh away the sin of the world (Jeremiah 31:33 and Hebrews 8:8-13). This New Covenant broke down the middle wall of partition between Jew and Gentile and opened the door of salvation so that all might enter by faith.

Why then did God choose the nation Israel? The primary purpose was that through them the Promised Seed of Abraham might come and bring blessing upon all nations and peoples of the world. Under God's care the Seed was carried within the nation for about 2000 years through times when it seemed that they could not possibly survive.

There were times in Israel's early history when, because of the sinfulness of the people, God Himself seemed to be tempted to destroy the entire nation and begin over again with Moses (Exodus 32:9-14). Satan must have felt satisfied that the Promised Seed could never come when Nebuchadnezzar destroyed the city of Jerusalem, laid waste the entire land and carried most of the survivors into captivity. But God raised up "His Shepherd," Cyrus, who conquered Babylon after 70 years and in fulfillment of Jeremiah 29:10 restored the believing remnant to the Land and ordered the rebuilding of the Temple of God in Jerusalem. When the wicked Haman succeeded in having the King of Persia order the destruction of all Jews in the empire, it seemed that Satan again was going to destroy the promised Seed. But Esther was raised up by God "for such a time as this" and was able to save her people, the Jews, and bring about the destruction of Haman.

Think too of the attempts made by Satan to destroy the promised Seed when Herod ordered the death of the infants in and around Bethlehem; when Jesus' own townspeople in Nazareth tried to end His life by throwing Him over the precipice; when the sudden storm on Galilee threatened to sink the boat in which Jesus was sleeping. No! The promised Seed was preserved until the hour when He made Himself an offering for the sin of the world and though on the cross He submitted voluntarily to the power of death, He came forth from the grave the mighty Victor over sin and forever has the keys of hell and death.

At last "in the fullness of time" God sent forth His Son, born of the virgin, the Seed of Abraham and of David according to the flesh. The Almighty had preserved the Chosen Nation in order that He might be born in Bethlehem, reared in Nazareth, minister in Galilee and Judea and finally die and rise again in the city of Jerusalem. It was God's plan of history gradually unfolded in the words of Scripture through the prophets that in this land and nation the great redemptive sacrifice would be accomplished. Over the Judean hilltop just outside the city wall, the deep darkness of sin's night gave way to the light of everlasting hope when the cry of the Saviour was heard from the cross, "It is finished!"

THE PLACE OF REDEMPTION

God not only needed a nation in which to cradle the Promised Seed and a nation where the great act of redemption could be carried out, He also needed a separate and distinct people in which He could reveal His almighty power as a witness to the nations of the world. To Israel was given the Holy Scriptures which tell the story of His mighty acts and through the prophets testified of the coming of the Messiah, the Hope of Israel and of the world. To Israel was given a great heritage of faith received from the fathers, Abraham, Isaac, and Jacob and from countless others who were loyal and obedient to the Word of God. In Israel God kept a remnant of those who believed so that, in spite of national idolatry, corruption, and flagrant rebellion, He preserved the nation's identity and continuity to the coming of the Messiah.

"Salvation is of the Jews" is true as our Lord Himself said (John 4:22). But salvation for Israel and the world is not of the Jews as a rebellious, unbelieving disobedient nation. It came through the true Seed of Abraham, Jesus the Messiah, and has been ministered through faithful believing Jewish prophets and apostles. We have only to look at history to see that it is the believing Israelite that has been God's witness, not the unbelieving nation. It is true that at times God blessed the nation as a whole and used Israel as a demonstration of His goodness and mercy before other nations, but this was only when Israel's leaders were loyal and obedient to God.

SALVATION THROUGH BELIEVING JEWS

Who was it that brought salvation to the world? Was it the nation that put Him on trial and shouted "Crucify Him" or was it the Messiah, the rejected King of the Jews, who hung upon Calvary's cross? Who carried the message of the Gospel to a needy, broken, sin-sick world? Was it the nation which tried to stop the preaching of the resurrection of Jesus and persecuted the early believers or was it the handful of humble believers who proclaimed the risen Lord and Saviour and would rather face prison and even death than disobey His command to preach the gospel to every creature?

Salvation is truly "of the Jews" and we are grateful to God for the blessings that have come to us through that nation. The Holy Scriptures came to us through prophets of Israel but they were true believers and were often rejected, persecuted or even killed by their own nation. Our only hope of righteousness has been provided for us by Jesus of Nazareth (a Jew by birth but at the same time God's only Son) and we are eternally grateful for such a Saviour, yet His own nation joined the Romans in putting Him upon a cross, "despised and rejected of men." The New Testament almost in its entirety was given to us by Jews and again we are thankful for their great contribution under God's Spirit; but they were ostracized from the Jewish synagogues of their own nation. The men who turned the world upside down in the first century by their preaching and teaching for the most part were Jews but the rulers of their nation sought to silence them by imprisonment or death. We thank God for every believing Jew who has by God's grace been an instrument of sharing the witness of salvation and everlasting hope with the world.

How beautifully God fulfilled the prophetic word of Zechariah by the preaching of the apostles, evangelists and other scattered Christian Jews in the first century. The prophet had foretold that in those days it shall come to pass that ten men shall take hold out of all languages of the nations, even shall take hold of the skirt of him that is a Jew, saying, 'We will go with you for we have heard that God is with you' (Zechariah 8:23).

Note that the Scofield Bible has a comment on "in those days" referring them to the yet future days when Jerusalem has been made the center of earth's worship and many follow this teaching.

But this is in direct contradiction to the clear teaching of Jesus that "neither in this mountain [in Samaria] nor yet at Jerusalem" shall men worship the Father (John 4:21):

But the hour cometh and now is when the true worshippers shall worship the Father in spirit and in truth: for the Father seeketh such to worship Him. God is a Spirit: and they that worship Him must worship Him in spirit and in truth (John 4:23,24).

Did Jesus mean that this spiritual worship would be only during a temporary dispensation or is He trying to tell us plainly that the worship that had for centuries been centered in Jerusalem was a shadow of the true worship of the Father in spirit in the "city of the living God, the heavenly Jerusalem" unto which we believers have already come (Hebrews 12:22)? The New Testament gives us a clear answer if we will hear it and we thank God that in His plan "salvation is of the Jews," through the Jewish Saviour-Messiah (God's only begotten Son) and through Jewish prophets, apostles and evangelists. Jerusalem already has been made the center of spiritual worship for the world since Jesus, the Messiah, suffered, died and rose again in that city.

ISRAEL'S FAILURE

And yet we must recognize the failure of the nation to be obedient to the revealed will of God and its often recurring cycles of disobedience, judgment, repentance, obedience and blessing. Their prophets condemned their idolatry, their dishonesty, their shallow worship and their sacrifices offered with guilty hands, which were an abomination to the Lord who desired of them that they should "do justly, and love mercy, and walk humbly with their God" (Micah 6:8). Their rebellious, disobedient spirit finally resulted in their total rejection of their own Messiah, who had come to redeem them from their sins.

How tragic was this awful denial! No one enjoys speaking of the part the Jewish nation had in the crucifixion of Jesus for it seems to anyone who is looking for an indication of anti-Semitism that the blame is placed upon a particular people and others are freed from any responsibility. Let me say very strongly that their part in the tragedy was only an evidence of the sinfulness of human nature which in its unredeemed state is at enmity against God. We all share in guilt because it was sin that nailed Him to the cross, my sin and your sin. "All have sinned and come short of the glory of God" (Romans 3:23). "All we like sheep have gone astray, we have turned every one to his own way and the Lord hath laid on Him the iniquity of us all" (Isaiah 53:6). But the fact that all mankind, because of sin, is responsible for the death of the Lamb of God, does not mean that the ones who actually took part in the trial and public execution of the Messiah were held guiltless by God. Certainly not.

Do you imagine that Pontius Pilate was not held accountable before God for the violation of his own conscience when he sentenced to death by crucifixion a man whom he himself judged to be innocent? Did not the Almighty bring about the destruction of the Roman Empire that had participated in the crucifixion of Jesus within four centuries after His death? Have not nineteen centuries of the history of the wanderings of a homeless Jewish race been sufficient evidence of His judgment upon them?

They had said, "His blood be upon us and our children" (Matthew 27:25). St. Paul said, "The wrath is come upon them to the uttermost" (I Thessalonians 2:16). And the Lord Jesus said,

> That upon you may come all the righteous blood shed upon the earth from the blood of righteous Abel unto the blood of Zecharias, son of Berachias, whom ye slew between the temple and the altar. Verily I say unto you, All these things shall come upon this generation.... Behold, your house is left unto you desolate (Matthew 23:35-38).

78

JUDGMENT

The great day of judgment on the nation of Israel came in 70 A.D. when the city of Jerusalem fell into the hands of Titus, the Roman general. The temple was destroyed, most of the population died by the sword or by famine and those taken alive were sent into slavery. How clearly this fulfilled the prophecy of Zechariah 14:1 and 2:

> Behold, the day of the Lord cometh, and thy spoil shall be divided in the midst of thee. For I will gather all nations against Jerusalem to battle: and the city shall be taken, and the houses rifled, and the women ravished; and half of the city shall go forth into captivity and the residue of the people shall not be cut off from the city.

Notice it is God who brings the nations against Jerusalem in judgment and certainly the Roman Empire represented all nations in 70 A.D., the day of the Lord's judgment on Israel.

But the judgment of blindness also had been put upon the nation and that blindness has continued through nineteen centuries unto this day. Except for a comparative few who individually have believed in Jesus as their Saviour and Lord, the majority of Jews have either clung to their traditions under the Old Covenant of the Mosaic law or have rejected in part or entirely any acceptance of personal religious conviction and beliefs.

This is in spite of the plain declaration of the prophet Jeremiah that the Mosaic Covenant had failed and God would make a New Covenant, a spiritual one, with the House of Israel (Jeremiah 31:31-34). One would think that surely a people who consider themselves the chosen people of God would wonder why, for nineteen hundred years, He had allowed them to suffer so much. Why would God, who had shown His power in the deliverance of His people through centuries of history before the Christian era, permit them, in these past centuries, to suffer in so many nations and finally to such a degree in Hitler's Germany? The only reasonable answer is that the same God, who used the Assyrians and Babylonians to punish Israel for her stubborn rebellion and willful disobedience 25 centuries ago, used the Roman army in 70 A.D. to punish the nation for its continued willful rejection of His Son. It was a tragic and terrible sin to crucify God's Son and the judgment upon the nation has likewise been terrible.

WITH MERCY

As he brought judgment on Israel, we might ask, "Did God cast away His people?" No, surely not! Had not God's Son prayed with infinite love from His cross, "Father, forgive them for they know not what they do"? St. Paul answers that question in Romans 11:1ff, exhibiting himself as a redeemed Jew brought nigh to God through faith in Christ. God opened the door wide on the day of Pentecost and on that day three thousand Jews and proselytes responded to the gospel preaching. Daily other Jews believed and came into the fellowship; on another day 5000 were added and later we read, "And the number of the disciples multipled greatly in Jerusalem and a great company of the priests were obedient to the faith." No! God did not cast away His people.

The Christian church began in Jerusalem with thousands of Jews who repented and believed and the door of salvation has always been open to any who believe, whether Jew or Gentile. God waited before He administered judgment upon Israel until the cup of iniquity was full and the nation was found guilty, not only of refusing to enter the kingdom of God, but also trying to keep the Gentiles from entering (I Thessalonians 2:14-16). This was the climax of sin against the grace of God by a nation called and chosen to bring blessing to the whole world. Nevertheless, in spite of the nation's rebellion, God had brought salvation to a broken, needy world through His Beloved Son, the Jewish Messiah and shared the message with all nations through believing Jewish prophets, apostles and evangelists. His Word could not fail. He had promised to Abraham that in His Seed all nations should be blessed and with the confirming of the New Covenant with the house of Israel, He fulfilled His Word.

EXIT OLD COVENANT

Until the New Covenant was confirmed by the Messiah,

Israel nationally was God's chosen instrument of witness to the world with the commandments, the scriptures, the prophets, the temple and priestly system, the sacrifices, the feasts and a strict Sabbath observance. Any Gentiles had to become proselytes to share in Israel's blessings. The New Covenant erased the distinction between Jew and Gentile in the process of salvation, broke down the barriers and opened a new and living way into the presence of God simply by faith in the Messiah. The temple in Jerusalem was no longer necessary because Jesus had made it possible for any believer to come directly into God's presence; the sacrifices ceased because the perfect sacrifice was offered by the Great High Priest once and for all; the feasts no longer need be observed because Jesus the Messiah was their fulfillment; the promised blessing through Abraham's Seed had come upon Jew and Gentile alike and the Gospel was to be preached to every creature.

There are some who fail to realize that when the New Covenant prophesied by Jeremiah was confirmed by the Messiah, the Old Mosaic Covenant was done away. This is clearly taught in Hebrews, chapter 8, and was vividly realized in history when the Roman army under Titus destroyed Jerusalem and the temple. Israel was no longer under the Mosaic Covenant as the chosen nation. She was brought under the New Covenant which was sealed with the precious blood of Christ and from that day on together with all the nations of the earth, Israel must respond to the preaching of the Gospel in order to receive everlasting life.

Did God then cast away His people? Will He begin again to deal with Israel as a nation? Is He through with the nation or does He have something in His plan that is yet to be fulfilled? I believe that He has and that He is even now making preparations for the outpouring of His love and mercy upon His chosen nation, Israel. Some would like to deny this and think that God was through with the Jew nationally nineteen centuries ago. But in order to sustain their position (1) they must ignore the amazing fact of God's providence in preserving them as a distinct people through nineteen hundred years of wandering and exile, scattered among the nations without a homeland; (2) they must ignore the plain fact that God's providence in this century has allowed them, even though still rebellious and unbelieving, to establish a State in their former homeland; and (3) they must disregard the evidence of God's continued heavy hand upon them in judgment and in the sustained judgmental "blindness in part" placed upon them for 1900 years. God certainly has not forgotten them nor ceased to deal with them.

WHY RESTORATION?

He has restored them to the land even though they have gathered to their "homeland" in unbelief and have established and maintained an independent Jewish State by four wars. This evidently has been allowed by God to bring to fulfillment the prophetic words of Jesus uttered nineteen centuries ago, which foretold the end of Gentile domination over Jerusalem. Amazing proof of the deity of Jesus and His divine fore-knowledge! But what is the purpose of this restoration of Israel to their homeland?

Marvin J. Rosenthal, Executive Director of The Friends of Israel Gospel Ministry, Inc., has this to say of God's dealing with Israel, and I quote:

> Israel was God's covenant people in the Old Testament. She was in the place of special privilege and blessing. Her greatest Son was Jesus the Messiah. In the fullness of time He came unto His own and, officially, the nation received Him not. Israel was nationally set aside and at Pentecost the Church, composed of believing Jews and Gentiles, was established. Today it is the true Church which stands in the place of special relationship with God. When the Church is raptured (caught up to be with the Lord, I Thessalonians 4:13-18), God will again begin dealing with Israel as a national entity.*

This kind of teaching seems to assume that during the entire church age Israel was nationally set aside and God only begins dealing with Israel as a national entity after the Church is removed by the rapture. His teaching ignores completely the fact that the New Covenant was confirmed with the House of Israel at Calvary with a perfect sacrifice that caused the sacrifices of Israel to cease since they were

*Israel, My Glory, Vol. 37, No. 1, Feb./Mar. 1979, p. 5.

fulfilled in the one supreme sacrifice of Jesus. It ignores the fact that the Church in the first few years of its existence was entirely Jewish, proving that the covenant of salvation was made with them. It ignores the fact that all through the church age God still has been dealing with the nation though scattered and homeless for He has preserved it and kept it from extinction while holding it under His hand of judgment. And what seems to me most tragic is that it offers no opportunity for Israel, after the blindness is removed from the nation, to have the privilege of the natural (Jewish) branches (Romans 11) being grafted back into their own household of faith, the present Church, enjoying the blessing of salvation. St. Paul makes it clear in Romans 11 that if they remain not in unbelief, they will be grafted in again. If the blindness is not removed until after the rapture of the Church, then there will be no Church to which they can be grafted back in and Paul's statement is meaningless.

I believe it is more true to the Scriptures to recognize that the Old Covenant with Israel failed because it was of the Law and that now there is no covenantal relationship between God and Israel except that which was sealed and confirmed at Calvary. It is impossible to conceive that God would restore a covenantal relationship of law that He Himself declared had failed (Jeremiah 31:31). The law and the ritual was a shadow of the reality that Jew and Gentile would find in the Lord Jesus. The present covenantal relationship was made with both Jew and Gentile, in Him. Note carefully that the covenant was made first with the Jew but provided for the inclusion of the Gentile. Jesus sent the disciples into the world with the gospel but they were to begin at Jerusalem, then go to Judea, then to Samaria and to the whole world (Acts 1:8). Note too that while we call it the New Covenant because it was sealed at Calvary, in reality it was confirmed (with Abraham) over 400 years before the Mosaic covenant (see Galatians 3:17,18).

When God says that the middle wall of partition was broken down, how can we imagine that God will build again that wall and establish or reestablish another covenant with the natural seed of Abraham? It is so contrary to the clear teaching of Scripture which says that "they which are the children of the flesh, these are not the children of God; but the children of the promise are counted for the seed"

(Romans 9:8). The children of the flesh had to believe if they were to be counted as the true seed of Abraham. And Scripture teaches both in Romans and Galatians that Gentiles who truly believe in the Messiah are likewise counted as Abraham's seed.

GREATEST BLESSING

God's greatest blessing upon Israel as a nation will not be given by making them the leading nation of the world with all the pomp and ceremony and power that appeals to the flesh. Rather His blessing will come upon that nation when in mercy He removes the judgment of *blindness* from their eyes and enables them through their own Scriptures to see that Jesus of Nazareth is the Messiah, the Son of the living God who died for them and rose again that they might live in His righteousness.

Think what it will be when the great majority of Jews are made alive in Christ and become members of the household of faith, the final capstone of the Temple which He is building, the completion of the Bride of Christ ready to meet the Saviour when He comes again. What rejoicing there will be throughout the Church when Israel takes its place under the banner of the cross and joins the hosts of believers of every nation in ascribing praise and dominion and power unto Him that sitteth upon the throne! Will you pray for that glorious day to come?

CHAPTER VI

Israel's Covenant Through David

For TWO VERY IMPORTANT REASONS, it is necessary that we spend time in carefully examining the promise of God to David and his house in II Samuel 7:16: "And thine house and thy kingdom shall be established forever before thee: thy throne shall be established forever." First, there is wide disagreement as to whether this prophecy was fulfilled when Jesus came long ago. And second, there are opposite opinions as to whether this prophecy was meant to be taken literally or spiritually.

JACOB'S PROPHECY

To preface this study, we need to go back to the first mention of a king in Israel found in Genesis 49:8-10. Jacob in this chapter pronounces his blessing upon his sons and says of Judah, "The sceptre shall not depart from Judah nor a lawgiver from between his feet, until Shiloh come; and unto him shall the gathering of the people be" (Genesis 49:10). Thus Jacob prophesies that Judah should be the royal tribe and that one from the tribe of Judah should hold the sceptre and give forth the laws for God's people.

This was fulfilled when David ascended to the throne about 750 years later. Note that the sceptre would not depart from Judah until Shiloh (commonly understood to refer to the Messiah) should come but at that time there would be a transfer of authority and the gathering of the people would be to Him. This teaches that when the Messiah came, the sceptre was transferred to His hand and the people either of the nation or of the nations of the world would become His subjects. Think of how this prophecy given by Jacob was so wonderfully fulfilled in David's royal house and supremely in Jesus, Son of David, at His coming.

BALAAM'S PROPHECY

Next we turn to Numbers 23:21 where we read the words of Balaam, who was hired by King Balak to curse the children of Israel. But he said,

> Behold, I have received commandment to bless: and He hath blessed; and I cannot reverse it. He hath not beheld iniquity in Jacob, neither hath He seen perverseness in Israel: the Lord his God is with him and the shout of a king is among them.

Israel did not have a king for several hundred years after this prophecy was uttered. Do we doubt that the shout he heard was the shout not of David but of David's greater Son, the Messiah? Again, in Numbers 24:17-19 we have great prophetic words from the mouth of Balaam as God controlled his spirit.

> I shall see him but not now: I shall behold him but not nigh; there shall come a Star out of Jacob, and a Sceptre shall rise out of Israel, and shall smite the corners of Moab and destroy all the children of Sheth. And Edom shall be a possession, Seir also shall be a possession for his enemies: and Israel shall do valiantly. Out of Jacob

shall come he that shall have dominion and shall destroy him that remaineth of the city.

This undoubtedly was fulfilled partially by David, the type of the Messiah King, who did conquer the enemies of Israel but it is completely fulfilled by Jesus, Son of David, in His world-wide dominion and possession of peoples of all nations. Most commentators agree that Balaam was announcing the coming of the Messiah, the Lord Jesus.

In Deuteronomy, the Lord, through Moses, foretells that Israel will want a king like all the nations around them and instructs them as to the kingship. He must be one chosen by God among his people. He should not multiply horses, wives, or silver and gold; he should have a copy of God's law and should read in it all the days of his life; and he should keep a humble heart and obey God's commandments (Deuteronomy 17:14-20). How tragic that Solomon, Israel's wisest and most illustrious king, should disobey in the three specific prohibitions regarding multiplying horses, wives and riches and that ten of the twelve tribes of Israel were torn from the kingdom at his death.

REJECTING GOD'S RULE

Finally, in I Samuel 8:4-5, we have the request of the people to Samuel that he make a king to rule Israel like all the nations. The idea of a king displeased the great judge of Israel so he went to the Lord in prayer. But God answered Samuel and said,

> Hearken unto the voice of the people in all that they say unto thee: for they have not rejected thee, but they have rejected Me, that I should not reign over them (I Samuel 8:7).

How plain are these words in telling us that the whole idea of an earthly king over Israel was a rejection of God's rule by His own chosen nation. This rejection culminated a thousand years later at the trial of Jesus in Jerusalem when they cried out, "We have no king but Caesar" (John 19:15b).

Now we learn from the passages presented above several important things.

1. The tribe of Judah would have the sceptre in Israel for a limited time—until Shiloh come.

2. Israel would produce a King who would have dominion and to Him would the people gather.

3. Israel's king would be God-appointed and would keep the revealed law of God.

4. For Israel to desire an earthly kingdom, like other nations, was a rejection of God's rule over them.

Still we find that after rejecting Israel's first king chosen from the tribe of Benjamin, God raised up "a man after God's own heart" to sit upon the throne and gave him victory over all the enemies of Israel. God also promised that He would establish David's house and kingdom forever. Even if David's descendants should sin, God would chasten them but would not take away His mercy from them as He took it away from King Saul. And He kept His Word through all the generations down to the coming of Christ, the Messiah, even through years of exile and captivity and through centuries when Israel was under Gentile government. Always God preserved the seed of David's house and the promise of the everlasting kingdom. Surely Israel was wrong in imagining that Messiah's kingdom would be a kingdom of this world. Didn't they realize that their desire for a kingdom like other nations with power and authority was a rejection of God's rule over them? Today many have fallen into the same false hope of an earthly kingdom with King Jesus sitting on a throne in Jerusalem ruling the nations with a rod of iron and dashing them in pieces like a potter's vessel during a thousand years on this earth. Why do men believe that Jesus has to have a worldly kingdom for a thousand years to fulfill prophecy? The kingdom promised to the Messiah is an "everlasting" kingdom, not limited to 1000 years. David's earthly royal line could never be maintained in a worldly kingdom forever in the sense of everlasting and history has proved that it wasn't.

Look at the history of the Kingdom of Israel after God granted their request and allowed them to have a king. (1) He gave them Saul as their first king, a type of man's choice, head and shoulders above his fellows, but Saul was disobedient and failed to trust in God and consequently was set aside, his whole house being removed from royal privilege. (2) Then God chose David, a shepherd boy, to take his place and anointed him to rule His people. He was "a man after God's own heart" and by trusting God and obeying His commandments he was made victorious over the enemies of Israel, extending his authority to the River Euphrates. David was a type of the Messiah who should "possess the gate of His enemies" and conquer the powers of darkness and of Hell. (3) David reigned for forty years and then his son, Solomon, took the throne. He inherited a kingdom that was firmly established by his father so he could reign in peace and build the temple in Jerusalem for the worship of God. Thus he was a type of the Prince of Peace in whom are hid all the treasures of wisdom and knowledge, who has built the spiritual temple of living stones and who holds the wealth of the world in His hands. The splendor and renown of Solomon's kingdom was a poor shadow of the everlasting kingdom of the One, greater than Solomon, whose glory out-shines the sun and will continue to shine through all the ages to come. (4) Solomon reigned for forty years and because of his transgressions the kingdom was rent asunder, ten tribes forming the kingdom of Israel and two tribes remaining loyal to the house of David in the Kingdom of Judah. God kept the Davidic line on the throne of Judah for 400 years before He sent them into exile in the Babylonian captivity, but the northern kingdom of Israel was a disastrous failure, existing for less than three short centuries with not one king who "did that which was right in the sight of the Lord." (5) There was only One who could restore the house of David and that was the child of Bethlehem, of David's seed who fulfilled the prophecy of Isaiah 9:6,7:

> For unto us a child is born, unto us a son is given, and the government shall be upon his shoulder: and his name shall be called Wonderful, Counsellor, The Mighty God, The Everlasting Father, The Prince of Peace. Of the increase of his government and peace there shall be no end, upon the throne of David, and upon his kingdom to order it and to establish it with judgment and with justice from henceforth and even forevermore. The zeal of the Lord of Hosts will perform this.

Notice carefully and underscore it in your mind that He came not to reestablish an earthly kingdom under the rule of David's house but to be a Saviour, to provide forgiveness of sins, to deliver from the fear of death, to give knowledge of salvation and to establish His everlasting Kingdom over all who would receive Him. Compare the great prophecy of Zacharias who was filled with the Holy Spirit in Luke 1:67-79. Some will quote the Angel's words to Mary:

> He shall be great and shall be called the Son of the Highest: and the Lord God shall give unto Him the throne of His father David: And He shall reign over the House of Jacob forever; and of His kingdom there shall be no end (Luke 1:32,33).

They will maintain that this has to be literally fulfilled on this earth in a millennial kingdom and since it has not been so fulfilled, it still will be in the future. We might agree if the Angel had said, "He shall reign over the House of Jacob for a thousand years" but the annunciation speaks of a different kind of reign—a reign lasting forever with no end to His Kingdom. That certainly is not a prophecy of an earthly, millennial kingdom and is much more in accord with the revelation of the Kingdom of God's dear Son, which has already been established and will continue forever.

JESUS THE TRUE KING

At the beginning of His earthly life, Jesus was acclaimed by the Wise Men from the East to be the King of the Jews and at the close when He was lifted on a cross to die, He was declared by the superscription above His thorn-crowned brow in three languages to be Jesus of Nazareth, King of the Jews. How wonderfully God was fulfilling all prophecy in Him.

Jesus Himself said plainly that His Kingdom was not of this world.

> Jesus answered, My Kingdom is not of this world: if my kingdom were of this world, then would my servants fight, that I should not be delivered to the Jews: but now is my Kingdom not from hence (John 18:36).

All of our Lord's teaching made it clear that the Kingdom of Jesus was a different kind of kingdom from the kingdoms of the world. His Kingdom was to be established in the hearts of men who would surrender unconditionally to His Lordship. His Kingdom was to be spread throughout the world by sowing the seed of the Word of God (Matthew 13). The resurrected Jesus taught His disciples and they went everywhere preaching the Kingdom of God (see Acts 1:3, 8-12; 20:25 and 28:23). Everyone who believed, whether Jew or Gentile, was "delivered from the power of darkness and translated into the kingdom of His dear Son" (Colossians 1:13). When Jesus was asked by the mother of Zebedee's sons if He would grant them the place on the right and on the left beside Him in His Kingdom, Jesus revealed that such personal ambition for position and authority was altogether out of harmony with the standard of His Kingdom. Jesus called the disciples to Him and said,

> Ye know that the princes of the Gentiles exercise dominion over them and they that are great exercise authority upon them. But it shall not be so among you: but whosoever will be great among you, let him be your minister; and whosoever will be chief among you, let him be your servant: Even as the Son of Man came not to be ministered unto but to minister and to give His life a ransom for many (Matthew 20:25-28).

THREE TEXTS MISUNDERSTOOD

Some Bible teachers catch on to the phrase in John 18:36, "But now is my kingdom not from hence" emphasizing the word "now" and implying that later our Lord's Kingdom would be a worldly kingdom and His servants would then fight for Him. I believe, however, that the word "now" is used in relation to Israel's past history, the centuries when the nation had fought against the Gentiles and was still hoping to throw off Roman tyranny by using the sword. Now that Israel's true King had come, the Prince of Peace, who would speak peace unto the heathen (see Zechariah 9:9,10) and who by the blood of the cross made peace reconciling both Jew and Gentile unto God in one body—now that He had come, those of His Kingdom would not take up the sword to defend Him. He needs no defense for He is the Mighty Conqueror.

Again, some teachers do not take seriously the word of Jesus to the Jewish leaders found in Matthew 21:43, "Therefore I say unto you, the kingdom of God shall be taken from you, and given to a nation bringing forth the fruits thereof." Without any warrant they simply say that this means that Christ was going to take the kingdom from the present wicked leaders of Israel and then give it back at a later date and it would be a Jewish kingdom restored for the millennium. If we are to deal fairly with these words of Jesus, we must consider their meaning in the light of the parable just preceding them. In verses 33-41 of this chapter 21 of Matthew, Jesus told the parable of the wicked husbandmen who slew the son of the owner of the vineyard. Plainly He was foretelling what the leaders of Israel would do to Him and in verse 41 He leads them to condemn themselves to destruction. Then it is that Jesus tells them that the kingdom would be taken from them and given to a nation bringing forth fruit. To whom was the kingdom given? Let the Saviour answer. "Fear not little flock, for it is the Father's good pleasure to give you the kingdom" (Luke 12:32).

Another text misused by many Bible teachers is Acts 1:6-8:

> When they therefore were come together they asked of Him saying 'Lord, wilt thou at this time restore the Kingdom to Israel?' And He said unto them, 'It is not for you to know the times or the seasons, which the Father hath put in His own power. But ye shall receive power after that the Holy Ghost is come upon you and ye shall be witnesses unto me....

They take Jesus' answer to the question of the disciples to be an implied acknowledgment that the kingdom someday will be restored to Israel again, but Jesus does not say that it will be restored at some future time. The very question asked by the disciples revealed that they didn't understand at all the purposes of the Father. He had not even taken the kingdom from Israel at that time and would not for some forty years. They didn't understand what the kingdom really was or when and how it was being established and they wouldn't know until they were taught by the Holy Spirit.

THE TRUE KINGDOM

When the Holy Spirit came upon them they witnessed concerning Jesus and preached the things pertaining to the Kingdom of God. St. Paul learned what the Kingdom of God is and tells us clearly in Romans 14:17, "For the Kingdom of God is not meat and drink; but righteousness and peace and joy in the Holy Ghost." The kingdom was no longer to be a Jewish kingdom of this world like the other nations have. It was to be a world-wide empire ruled by the law of love, speaking peace to all who would submit to Jesus as Lord and receive Him as Saviour. It was a kingdom that began with a handful of Jewish believers who accepted their crucified and risen Lord as the King of Kings and Lord of Lords and spread by the "foolishness" of preaching until people of every race and nation have bowed the knee to Christ. Some day it will be true that "at the Name of Jesus every knee shall bow and every tongue confess that Jesus Christ is Lord to the glory of God the Father." He is reigning now until all His enemies are put under His feet (I Corinthians 15:25) and for these 1900 years since His resurrection He has been exercising all authority in heaven and on earth (Matthew 28:18).

We conclude then that Jesus was of the seed of David, the royal house of Judah and that He came to be not only Saviour but King. His Kingdom is infinitely greater than a mere restoration of royalty to the Jewish nation leading them to deliverance from Roman tyranny. He came to win the allegiance of the hearts of men by His love and sacrifice and would bring Jew and Gentile through faith in Him into one body, one kingdom, including people of every tribe and kindred and tongue and nation, all joined together in Him under the banner of His lovel. Israel's desire for a king and kingdom like the other nations was a rejection of the sovereignty of God. The desire for a king who would break the yoke of Rome which was so heavy on the neck of Judah was of the same spirit and caused Israel to miss the day of visitation when the Saviour offered them His love and grace. I fear that the same spirit is revealed among many evangelical Christians who look for Israel's national restoration to worldly power and glory and who care little for Israel's present hope of salvation and her being grafted back into the true vine as a part of Christ's body, His Church. (See also

Matthew 13:24-30 and 36-43. It is very clear that the church will be left until the "end of the world" when the harvest will be gathered. Jesus claimed the world as His Kingdom!)

CHAPTER VII

Israel's Captivity and Return

HOW CLEARLY WE SEE GOD revealed as the Lord of history and the sovereign of all nations as we study the Scriptures that relate to the 70-year captivity of the nation of Israel. More than this, we see Him as the Saviour who takes no pleasure in the death of the wicked and who pleads for His people to repent of their sins and trust in Him.

How tragic that He should have to bring judgment upon the land and the people whom He had chosen to be an instrument of His blessing to the nations of the earth. Israel as a nation had proved herself to be a rebellious, sinful people throughout her history from the days of the wanderings in the wilderness until the captivity of Judah and Jerusalem in 586 B.C. God could not allow such a witness to continue any longer and in His righteousness brought "the weapons of His indignation to destroy the whole land" (Isaiah 13:5). He sent His prophets to foretell the doom that was coming and to call the nation to righteousness and obedience, but their answer to His servants again and again was mockery, imprisonment, stoning or even death.

The God of Israel had revealed Himself as

> The Lord, the Lord God, merciful and gracious, long suffering and abundant in goodness and truth, keeping mercy for thousands, forgiving iniquity and transgression and sin, and that will by no means clear the guilty: visiting the iniquity of the fathers upon the children and upon the children's children into the third and fourth generation (Exodus 34:6,7).

He revealed his patience with Israel by forebearing their rebellion and forgiving them again and again, but He must also be righteous in His judgment upon sin and upon sinners who continued to reject His word and grace. At last the day of judgment came which resulted in the cleansing of the land and a new start with a remnant of believers who trusted God after seventy years of captivity.

The Kingdom of Israel reached the zenith of its glory and power under the reign of David and then of Solomon, who together reigned for a total of about 80 years from 1056-975 B.C. Because of Solomon's sins, the kingdom was broken by the rebellion of ten tribes under King Jeroboam with only Judah and Benjamin remaining loyal to Solomon's son, Rehoboam. Jeroboam, king of the northern Kingdom of Israel, led his people in sin, giving them a calf to worship, and the kings that followed him through some 250 years "did evil in the sight of the Lord." God sent His prophets to warn the northern Kingdom of the consequences of their sins and when they would not listen but only hardened their hearts, He brought Assyria in 722 B.C. to destroy the cities of Israel and take her people captive.

The southern Kingdom of Judah was spared at that time as there was evidence of repentance and trust with a genuine reform later under King Josiah. But in 606, Nebuchadnezzer captured Jerusalem, taking captives and some treasures back to Babylon. Through the next twenty years, especially during King Zedekiah's reign, God pled with the nation to repent and submit in obedience to His will but all His pleading through the prophets Ezekiel and Jeremiah was in vain and the holocaust came in 586 B.C. when the Babylonians destroyed the Temple and the city of Jerusalem.

The judgment on both the Northern and Southern Kingdoms became inevitable after they continued to despise the Word of God delivered by the prophets. God sent His messengers with warnings and with pleadings during at least three centuries in His loving mercy trying to bring the nation into the way of righteousness. But to no avail. Listen to God's denunciation of Judah and then hear His plea as Isaiah opens his prophecy against Israel.

Hear O Heavens: and give ear, O earth: for the Lord hath spoken: I have nourished and brought up children, and they have rebelled against me: The ox knoweth his owner, and the ass his master's crib: but Israel doth not know, my people doth not consider. Ah sinful nation, a people laden with iniquity, a seed of evil doers, children that are corrupters! they have forsaken the Lord, they have provoked the Holy One of Israel unto anger, they are gone away backward. Why should ye be stricken anymore? ye will revolt more and more. The whole head is sick, and the whole heart faint. From the sole of the foot even unto the head there is no soundness in it: but wounds, and bruises, and putrifying sores: they have not been closed, neither bound up, neither mollified with ointment. Your country is desolate, your cities are burned with fire: your land, strangers devour it in your presence, and it is desolate, as overthrown by strangers. And the daughter of Zion is left as a cottage in a vineyard, as a lodge in a garden of cucumbers, as a besieged city. Except the Lord of hosts had left unto us a very small remnant, we should have been as Sodom, and we should have been like unto Gomorrah (Isaiah 1:2-9).

And God's plea to His sinful people:

Wash you, make you clean: put away the evil of your doings from before mine eyes: cease to do evil: learn to do well: seek judgment, relieve the oppressed: judge the fatherless: plead for the widow. Come now, and let us reason together, saith the Lord: Though your sins be as scarlet, they shall be as white as snow: though they be red like crimson, they shall be as wool. If ye be willing and obedient, ye shall eat the good of the land (Isaiah 1:16-19).

Read also Ezekiel, chapter 5, as an example of the vivid way in which the prophets describe what God was going to do in Jerusalem and why.

Can you imagine the sorrow in the compassionate heart of the God of Israel when He saw the beautiful Temple built by Solomon go up in flames and the Beloved City leveled to the ground? But dear reader, that was nothing compared with the anguish He must have felt when He "laid the iniquity of us all" on His beloved Son and turned His face away as Jesus hung on the cross in darkness on the hill called the Place of the Skull. Don't ever complain of the judgment of God until you have listened to the cry from Calvary, "My God! My God! Why hast Thou forsaken Me?" Remember, He was there receiving the judgment on your sin.

The destruction and desolation of the cities and land of Israel and Judah was predicted in Leviticus as the climax of God's chastisement upon His disobedient people. Israel had been given strict laws regarding the keeping of her sabbaths as a sign that they were God's chosen people and they ignored God's commands. So in Leviticus 26:33ff, we read

> And I will scatter you among the heathen and will draw out a sword after you: and your land shall be desolate and your cities waste. Then shall the land enjoy her sabbaths, as long as it lieth desolate and ye be in your enemies' land, even then shall the land rest and enjoy her sabbaths. As long as it lieth desolate, it shall rest: because it did not rest in your sabbaths when ye dwelt upon it.

WHY THE CAPTIVITY?

Jeremiah prophesied that the land would have its rest for 70 years and then God would visit them and, as He says, "perform my good word toward you, in causing you to return to this place" (Jeremiah 29:10). How marvelously this was fulfilled when God brought destruction and judgment upon the Babylonian Empire and then moved the heart of Cyrus, the conqueror, to return the captives to Jerusalem and rebuild the Temple.

Did God have any further purpose in scattering Israel in captivity other than to punish them and give the land rest for

70 years? The punishment for the continued sinfulness of Israel was no doubt the primary cause of His bringing the army of Babylon against Jerusalem with such terrible slaughter and destruction but surely He accomplished other purposes through this judgment. The Sovereign of heaven and earth can make the wrath of man to praise Him and I can see several things He accomplished through the widespread captivity of His people: (1) He cleansed the land of the abomination of idolatry; (2) He provided a witness of His glory in every part of the great Babylonian empire (described in Nebuchadnezzar's dream as the Head of Gold); (3) He revealed His power to restore to life a nation that was dead; and (4) He used Israel's return to set forth prophecies of blessings that would come through the Messiah. Let us look at these briefly.

(1) He cleansed the land of the abomination of idolatry. This was one of the great sins of a nation that had been called as the people chosen by the Lord God, the One true God. Yet on the very day when God was giving them His commandments, even at the same time, Israel was worshipping the golden calf, and thus revealed the tendency to accept the idolatrous practices of surrounding kingdoms. They even made their first-born "pass through the fire" as sacrifices to heathen idols which God never commanded them to do. Listen to the voice of Ezekiel as he prophesies against the mountains of Israel.

> Ye mountains of Israel hear the word of the Lord God: Thus saith the Lord God to the mountains and to the hills, to the rivers and to the valleys: Behold, I, even I will bring a sword upon you and I will destroy your high places. And your altars shall be desolate and your images shall be broken: And I will cast down your slain men before your idols. And I will lay the dead carcasses of the children of Israel before their idols: and I will scatter your bones round about your altars. In all your dwelling places the cities shall be laid waste and the high places shall be desolate: that your altars may be laid waste and made desolate and your idols may be broken and cease and your images may be cut down and your works may be abolished. And the slain shall fall in the midst of you and ye shall know that I am the Lord (Ezekiel 6:3-7).

Read the parable of Aholah and Aholibah, representing Samaria and Jerusalem, in Ezekiel 23, and see what God thinks of these respective cities in their spiritual adultery with other nations. When the Remnant returned under God's hand from the 70-year captivity, we find that they had such a strong aversion to idolatry that they never were guilty of adopting heathen practices of worship again.

(2) God provided a witness throughout the Gentile nations when He scattered His people in captivity. What a beautiful testimony we discover as we read the life of Daniel, his loyalty to religious principles, his sterling character, his prayer life, his understanding of dreams and his belief in God and the prophecies of Scripture! What a testimony to Nebuchad-nezzar the three young Jews gave when they were loyal to their worship of the God of Israel and refused to bow before the image of the king, even though they were cast into the fiery furnace! What an experience the great Babylonian king went through when he was driven out to eat grass like an animal until he humbled his heart before God and was allowed back on the throne! No wonder he proclaimed far and wide:

Now I Nebuchadnezzar praise and extol and honour the King of heaven, all whose works are truth and his ways judgment: and those that walk in pride He is able to abase (Daniel 4:37).

What a testimony it was for Cyrus, the Mede, conqueror of Babylon, to publish the following proclamation throughout all his kingdom:

Thus saith Cyrus king of Persia, the Lord God of heaven hath given me all the kingdoms of the earth: and He hath charged me to build Him an house at Jerusalem which is in Judah. Who is there among you of all His people? His God be with him and let him go up to Jerusalem which is in Judah and build the house of the Lord God of Israel (He is the God) which is in Jerusalem. And whosoever remaineth in any place where he sojourneth, let the men of his place help him with silver and with gold and with goods and with beasts beside the free-will offering for the house of God that is in Jerusalem (Ezra 1:2-4).

What a testimony to the Gentile nations to have Jews in every city bring the songs of Zion, the knowledge of the laws of God and the witness of God's mercy even in judgment to the people around them! What a testimony to the Persian Empire when Esther became queen and saved her people by courageously revealing the plot of the wicked Haman. A few years later Artaxerxes issued from the Persian throne the second decree which allowed the descendants of Israel throughout his empire to return to Jerusalem and especially encouraged the beautifying of the Temple (see Ezra 7:11-26). The king even commanded that God's laws should be taught and those who would not follow them should be punished!

Thus, even though Jesus the Messiah did not come for several centuries, the witness was widespread through the descendants of the captives who did not return and there were synagogues in most cities that became the first pulpits as the apostles went everywhere in the first century A.D. preaching the Gospel. How wonderfully God turned His judgment on Israel into blessing for the nations of the earth! "That they may know that I am the Lord" echoes again and again from the lips of Isaiah, Jeremiah and Ezekiel. This was God's purpose in the judgment upon Israel and the scattering of so many in captivity.

(3) God revealed His power to restore to life a nation that was dead. Surely it seemed certain after the destruction of Jerusalem and the desolation of the land that the Kingdom of Judah was dead. Her kings and princes were prisoners, two-thirds of her people were dead and the rest were scattered in the captivity "in all the nations of the earth" (Jeremiah 15:4; 29:18). God had promised through many prophets a return to the land, but to the scattered captives it seemed hopeless, especially when the Temple and the Beloved City was destroyed. It was then that God gave Ezekiel the vision of the valley full of bones, "very many" and "very dry." When asked if these bones could live, the prophet answered "O Lord God thou knowest." He was told that God would join the bones, covering them with sinews, flesh and skin and the Breath would come upon them and make them live. This vision is interpreted to mean that those who were "dead" in captivity, cut off with no hope, would have their "graves" opened and would return to the land. Both Judah and the children of Israel would come back as one nation

with one king over them and they would have one Shepherd (Ezekiel 37:1-28). So the Lord plainly tells of the restoration to their land of His people who as a nation were dead and hopeless.

I firmly believe that God used Israel through the centuries to teach us important spiritual truths. He had plainly taught the great act of redemption from sin by the blood in delivering Israel from bondage in Egypt, the angel of death passing over the homes marked with the blood of the lamb. Now through the "death" and "resurrection" of the nation that was captive 70 years, He portrays the judgment of death upon sin and the new life He gives to those, the remnant of Israel, who will believe in Him. It was necessary to teach the spiritual lesson that the natural man must die in Christ and be raised to newness of life if he is to receive the inheritance promised through Abraham's Seed. Great as was the miracle of deliverance of the slaves from bondage in Egypt, it was a greater miracle of God's grace to raise up a nation that was dead and grant it a new life in the land He had given them. No wonder the prophet Jeremiah says,

> Therefore behold, the days come, saith the Lord, that it shall no more be said, the Lord liveth, that brought up the children of Israel out of the land of Egypt; but, the Lord liveth that brought up the children of Israel from the land of the north and from all the lands whither He had driven them (Jeremiah 16:14,15).

(4) God used Israel's return from captivity to set forth prophecies of blessings that would come through the Messiah. I believe that the promised return to the land was to preserve the True Seed within the nation until His Coming and that the future blessings glowingly pictured in the words of the prophets have to do primarily with the believing remnant and with God's salvation for the world proclaimed now through the Gospel of Jesus Christ. This is quite different from the interpretation of those who apply such prophecies not to the church but to national Israel in the millennial kingdom age when Jesus reigns on an earthly throne and ensures a thousand years of peace and glory to that nation.

In Isaiah 9:6,7, we read the great promise of the coming of Jesus in these familiar words,

For unto us a child is born, unto us a son is given: and the government shall be upon His shoulders: and His Name shall be called Wonderful, Counselor, The Mighty God, The Everlasting Father, The Prince of Peace. Of the increase of His government and peace there shall be no end, upon the throne of David and upon his kingdom to order it and to establish it with judgment and with justice from henceforth even forever. The zeal of the Lord of Hosts will perform this.

The Scofield Bible has a note (p. 721) which says, "The 'Throne of David' is a phrase as definite, historically, as 'Throne of the Caesars,' and as little admits of 'spiritualizing.'" This means that poor Jesus, rejected by His nation cannot sit upon the throne of David or experience the glory of His Kingdom until after the tribulation and the millennium begins. What a low view this gives of the government promised in this prophecy to the Son of God! In reality, when was the government placed upon His shoulder? Was it not when God raised Him from the grave that He was given all authority and power in heaven and earth? (Matthew 28:18). When was "the Kingdom of our Lord Jesus Christ" established into which Paul says we are translated? (Colossians 1:13). Did our Lord Jesus have nothing to do with the kingdom which He said would be taken from the nation of Israel (Matthew 21:43) and given to "the little flock," the remnant who believed in Him? Was not this the true Kingdom of glory and peace promised by the prophets and given to the Son by the Father to be returned when all His enemies are subject to Him? (I Corinthians 15:24). Isaiah had prophesied that "the zeal of the Lord of Hosts will perform this" and not all the powers of hell that gloated over His crucifixion nor even the rejection by His own nation could keep Him from the true Throne of David or His own Kingdom of righteousness and love.

Another passage is Isaiah, chapter 11, which illustrates the way in which the prophet's words can be falsely applied to the millennial Kingdom age rather than to the present work of Messiah's Kingdom in the world. The entire chapter is related by Dr. Scofield to the Davidic Kingdom that is yet to be set up on this earth (Scofield Bible, Isaiah 11). However, this is shown to be false by the interpretation of God's own words in Romans 15:12: "And again, Esaias saith, There shall be a root of Jesse and He that shall rise to reign over the Gentiles; in Him shall the Gentiles trust." There Paul quotes the words of Isaiah 11:10, "And in that day there shall be a root of Jesse which shall stand for an ensign of the people: to it shall the Gentiles seek: and His rest shall be glorious." He applied them to the Gentiles who had found their hope in Christ. If God's Word explicitly applies the prophecy to the present Kingdom of Christ, which for 1900 years has included the Gentiles, why should anyone try to force a different application of the prophecy to a future millennial kingdom?

ENTER NEW COVENANT

It was in connection with the promised return of the remnant from captivity that Jeremiah gives the prophecy of the New Covenant God would make with the House of Israel.

> Behold the days come, saith the Lord, that I will make a new covenant with the house of Israel and with the house of Judah: Not according to the covenant that I made with their fathers in the day that I took them by the hand to bring them out of the land of Egypt; which covenant they brake, although I was an husband unto them, saith the Lord: But this shall be the covenant that I will make with the house of Israel; After those days, saith the Lord, I will put my law in their inward parts, and write it in their hearts; and I will be their God, and they shall be my people. And they shall teach no more every man his neighbor and every man his brother, saying, Know the Lord: for they shall all know me from the least of them to the greatest of them, saith the Lord: for I will forgive their iniquity and I will remember their sin no more (Jeremiah 31:31-34).

There are some teachers who teach that this New Covenant has not yet been established with the House of Israel because the words, "And they shall teach no more every man his neighbor and every man his brother saying, Know the Lord: for they shall all know me from the least to the greatest" have never been fulfilled. However, in Hebrews 8:8-13, we have Jeremiah's words quoted as specifically being fulfilled and it is better for us to accept the obvious interpretation of the New Testament (that such knowledge of God can only be taught by the Holy Spirit, not by man), rather than to deny that it has been fulfilled.

Ezekiel's prophecy in chapter 11:19,20 certainly foretells the same New Covenant in these words:

> And I will give them one heart, and I will put a new spirit within you: and I will take the stony heart out of their flesh and will give them an heart of flesh: that they may walk in my statutes and keep my ordinances and do them: and they shall be my people and I will be their God.

These are the opening words of Isaiah, chapter 54:

> Sing O barren, thou that didst not bear, break forth into singing and cry aloud, thou that didst not travail with child: for more are the children of the desolate than the children of the married wife, saith the Lord (Isaiah 54:1).

They are quoted by the Apostle Paul in Galatians 4:27 and applied spiritually to the children of the heavenly city, the new Jerusalem above. Verse 13 of Isaiah 54 is quoted by our Lord in John 6:45:

> As it is written in the prophets, and they shall be all taught of God. Every man therefore that hath heard and hath learned of the Father, cometh unto me.

Our Lord is interpreting them to have a deep spiritual meaning: that no one can come to Him except the Father draw him and this surely applies not just to the children of the house of Israel, but to all who are drawn to Jesus of every race or nation. How important that we understand that the message of the prophets of Israel was not just for that nation but has to do with the promised blessings of the Seed of Abraham for all nations as well.

Now as we conclude this chapter, it is necessary to give a brief summary from the historical perspective. The destruction and captivity of the Northern Kingdom of Israel took place in 722 under the Assyrians. Nebuchadnezzar, King of Babylon, captured Jerusalem and took many captives in

606 B.C. Twenty years later he came again and destroyed the city, burning the beautiful Temple of Solomon and again took thousands of captives, leaving only a few poor people in the desolate land. After fifty years had passed, in 536 B.C., Cyrus the Mede conquered Babylon and issued a decree (Ezra 1:1-4) allowing the captives to return to Jerusalem and build God's House which was completed in 516 B.C., just seventy years after it was destroyed. In 457 B.C. Artaxerxes issued a decree (Ezra 7:11-26) urging all captives of Israel in all his empire to return to Jerusalem to beautify the Temple of God and do "whatsoever shall seem good to thee [Ezra] and to thy brethren." From this year on (457 B.C.), for the next 483 years, according to Daniel's prophecy of seventy weeks, they waited for the coming of Messiah and the seven-year period when He would confirm the covenant and fulfill God's great purpose of worldwide redemption. Let us turn now to Daniel's great prophecy and consider it in detail.

CHAPTER VIII

Israel's Destiny
Revealed Through Daniel

WE COME NOW to the consideration of the prophecy in Daniel 9:24-27 in which he records God's revelation of the destiny of the nation of Israel, Daniel's people. It is preceded by a very moving prayer of confession of the sins of Israel and an appeal to the Lord to forgive and to hear and respond to the nation's desolations. What a tremendous appeal he makes to God in these closing words of his prayer:

O Lord according to all Thy righteousness, I beseech Thee, let Thine anger and Thy fury be turned away from Thy city Jerusalem, Thy Holy mountain: because for our sins and for the iniquity of our fathers, Jerusalem and Thy people are become a reproach to all that are about us. Now, therefore, O our God, hear the prayer of Thy servant and his supplications and cause Thy face to shine upon Thy sanctuary that is desolate, for the Lord's sake. O my God, incline Thine ear and hear; open Thine eyes and behold our desolations, and the city

which is called by Thy name: for we do not present our
supplications before Thee for our righteousness, but for
Thy great mercies. O Lord, hear; O Lord forgive; O Lord,
hearken and do defer not for Thine own sake, O my God;
for Thy city and Thy people are called by Thy name
(Daniel 9:16-19).

Note, in the early part of this prayer that Daniel definitely
relates the Babylonian captivity to the prophecy of Moses
which was thus fulfilled.

It was when Daniel understood from his study of God's
Word, especially in the Book of Jeremiah, that God "would
accomplish seventy years in the desolation of Jerusalem"
(Daniel 9:2) that he poured out his heart in supplication that
God now would grant pardon and deliverance. This is one
passage the Lord laid on my heart that has compelled me to
the urgency of writing this book. In Jeremiah the Lord
measured seventy years for the duration of the desolation of
Jerusalem. In Romans 11, the Lord declares through the
Apostle Paul that "blindness in part is happened to Israel,
until the fullness of the Gentiles be come in" (Romans 11:25).
Just as Daniel was moved to plead Israel's need, so I pray God
that His Spirit will place a great burden of prayer upon
Christians everywhere that God will remove that judgmental
blindness from Israel that they may believe and be saved.
Some say, "Forget it; that will take place when they see Him
in His physical return," but I believe that after Jesus comes
for His Bride, the Church, it will be too late for the salvation
of which Paul is speaking and which was his heart's desire
for his kinsmen according to the flesh.

Let us return to Daniel 9. It was while Daniel was still
speaking in prayer that Gabriel came to him from God with
the revelation of this important truth concerning Israel. How
near God is when He can send from heaven His messenger
who arrives even before we have finished speaking! Note how
important the message is which Gabriel delivers to the
greatly beloved Daniel. Dr. A.C. Gabelein, a Bible commen-
tator who represents the general premillennial view of
prophecy, says that "the prophetic message Gabriel brought
from the throne of God to Daniel is perhaps the most
important, not only in the book of Daniel, but in the whole

Bible."* We agree perfectly on the importance of this prophecy but are far apart on the interpretation of all that God is revealing and we must carefully consider these four verses and try to understand what is really said.

Daniel 9:24

Seventy weeks are determined upon thy people and upon thy holy city, to finish the transgression, and to make an end of sins, and to make reconciliation for iniquity and to bring in everlasting righteousness and to seal up the vision and prophecy, and to anoint the most Holy.

It is first necessary to understand the period described by the words "seventy weeks." Most evangelical Bible scholars consider the word "week" to refer to seven years instead of days, and consequently we have a period of 490 years in which certain things are to be accomplished. The premillennial view does not take this period as a consecutive period of years but inserts the entire 1900 plus years of the church age between the 69th and 70th week. One can see that this immediately makes a tremendous difference in interpreting the meaning of this verse. If it is taken to be a period of seventy consecutive sevens, which is the literal and to me the obvious meaning, then the things that were to be accomplished within 490 years must have been accomplished by the Lord Jesus as His first coming. But on the other hand, if the long indeterminate gap of over 1900 years is to be inserted before the 70th week, then those things will not be accomplished, at least for still seven more years, and not until the Second Coming of our Lord.

Six great things were to be accomplished within the seventy weeks determined upon Daniel's people:

1. to finish the transgression
2. to make an end of sins
3. to make reconciliation for iniquity

---

*A.C. Gabelein, *The Prophet Daniel*, p. 129.

4. to bring in everlasting righteousness
5. to seal up the vision and prophecy
6. to anoint the most Holy.

The important question is, "Were they accomplished at the first coming of our Lord?"

1. Was the transgression finished? There is sufficient New Testament evidence to answer this. Our Lord said in His scathing denunciation of the leaders of Israel,

> Wherefore ye be witnesses unto yourselves that ye are the children of them which killed the prophets. Fill ye up then the measure of your fathers. Ye serpents ye generation of vipers, how can ye escape the damnation of hell? Wherefore I send unto you prophets and wise men and scribes; and some of them ye shall kill and crucify: and some of them shall ye scourge in your synagogues and persecute them from city to city. That upon you may come all the righteous blood shed upon the earth from the blood of righteous Abel unto the blood of Zacharias, son of Barachias whom ye slew between the temple and the altar. Verily I say unto you, all these things shall come upon this generation (Matthew 23:31-36).

The phrases "fill ye up then the measure" and "all the righteous blood shed upon the earth" certainly indicate that this is a climax of the transgression of Israel. The words of Jesus, spoken on a different occasion, "For these be the days of vengeance, that all things which are written may be fulfilled" (Luke 21:22) likewise indicate that the cup of iniquity was full.

Again, St. Paul, in speaking of the unbelieving Jews, says,

> Who both killed the Lord Jesus and their own prophets and have persecuted us and they please not God and are contrary to all men: forbidding us to speak to the Gentiles that they might be saved, to fill up their sins alway: for the wrath is come upon them to the uttermost (I Thessalonians 2:15,16).

Certainly the climax of Israel's transgression against the God who chose her and loved her as a people came when they demanded of Pilate the crucifixion of their Messiah and then persecuted the disciples of Jesus for preaching the Saviour's redeeming grace to the Gentiles. The first important thing to be accomplished in the 490-year period was consummated as a result of the crucifixion.

2. Did our Saviour make an end of sins when He died on the cross? If we mean that sin ceased and no more sins were committed after Jesus died, the answer obviously is "no." But we cannot take these words to mean that an actual end of sin will be made within the seventy-week period for sin will continue until the final rebellion of Satan is overthrown and the judgment is accomplished. The New Testament again interprets for us the fulfillment of these prophetic words. St. Paul says,

> Blotting out the handwriting of ordinances that was against us, which was contrary to us and took it out of the way, nailing it to His cross, and having spoiled principalities and powers, He made a shew of them openly, triumphing over them in it (Colossians 2:14-15).

An even stronger statement is made by the writer of Hebrews where he says, "...but now once in the end of the world hath He appeared to put away sin by the sacrifice of Himself" (Hebrews 2:26). John, the forerunner of the Messiah, pointed to Him and said, "Behold, the Lamb of God which taketh away the sin of the world" (John 1:29) and St. Paul said, "For sin shall not have dominion over you: for ye are not under the law but under grace" (Romans 6:14). Did Christ "put away sin," "take away the sin of the world," destroy its power, and crush the head of the serpent when He cried, "It is finished"? Or does Scripture teach that sin has not yet been defeated and Jesus will have to fight another battle to take away or make an end of sins? The answer is obvious. Our Lord fought the battle once, He met and defeated Satan once and for all and while He allows Satan a certain limited, controlled freedom, Jesus has held the keys of death and hell for the past 19 centuries (see Revelation 1:18). The battle against sin is done. Christ is the Eternal Victor.

3. Did our Saviour cover iniquity when He came long ago? Surely there ought not to be a difference of interpretation in

our answer to this. I am confident that every honest Bible scholar recognizes that Jesus came to redeem us with His precious blood (I Peter 1:18,19), that He "came not to be ministered unto but to minister and to give His life a ransom for many" (Matthew 20:28), and that "He is the propitiation for our sins; and not for ours only but also for the sins of the whole world" (I John 2:2). It is sad, however, to find many who hold a view which claims that this was not accomplished for Israel and, therefore, the 490 years is extended by the church age and Gabriel's words will be fulfilled after the great tribulation.

These scholars fail to see that what Jesus did on the cross was done primarily to save and redeem His people, but also included the whole world. The gospel on the day of Pentecost was first preached to Jews and they were the first to know the forgiving grace of the Lord Jesus and to partake of His victory over sin. But these things that were to be accomplished according to the prophecy given Daniel do not concern Daniel's people exclusively. They undoubtedly refer to the work of the Messiah who was promised to bring blessing to all nations of the earth. When the angel announced His birth to the shepherds, he said, "Fear not, for behold, I bring you good tidings of great joy which shall be to all people" (Luke 2:10). What a tragedy it would have been if he had said "to all Jews" instead. Yet we are told by some that in this prophecy of the destiny of Daniel's people the great accomplishments to be performed have only and exclusively to deal with Jews. This is a narrow view of the Saviour of the world! and I thank God that the New Testament teaches otherwise!

4. Did Jesus Christ bring in everlasting righteousness? Perhaps the best answer is given by the Apostle Paul when he says,

> Therefore as by the offence of one [Adam] judgment came upon all men to condemnation: even so by the righteousness of one the free gift came upon all men unto justification of life. For as by one man's disobedience many were made sinners, so by the obedience of one shall many be made righteous (Romans 5:18,19).

Some apply this to a yet future time and look forward to the day when, in the millennial kingdom, Jesus shall reign in righteousness. This is simply to ignore the teaching of Scripture that our righteousness is as filthy rags but that Christ has already provided a righteousness for all who believe in Him. Today, we stand righteous in His sight if we trust Christ for He is made unto us "wisdom and righteousness." His perfect righteousness is imputed to our account through faith and we stand justified by grace. Jesus brought in perfect righteousness that is everlasting because He was perfect in obedience to His Father's will and I thank God that neither Jew nor Gentile has to wait for our Lord to do something more to "bring in everlasting righteousness."

5. Did our Lord seal up the vision and prophecy? He said plainly that He came not to destroy the law or the prophet but to fulfill (Matthew 5:17). He gave His Spirit to the disciples promising that He would guide them into all truth. Theirs were the last writings included in the Holy Scriptures and they all testify of Jesus who brought God's final Word to this sinful, rebellious world. The Old Covenant given to Israel through Moses was to be sealed up as a completed, fulfilled covenant which was to pass away and be replaced by the New Covenant given by our Lord, a better and the one true Mediator. Therefore, by His coming to reveal God's love and power through His words, His miracles, His sinless life and His death and resurrection, our Lord fulfilled the Old Covenant and sealed up the vision and prophet by instituting the New Covenant which was sealed by the Holy Spirit and confirmed by the sacrifice of Himself on Calvary.

An interesting fact regarding the two great books of prophecy, Daniel and Revelation, is found with respect to the way the timing of their events is handled. Daniel wrote his book somewhere around 536 B.C. and recorded explicit events that would happen during the second century B.C., culminating in the fulfillment of the destiny of His people and the coming of Messiah more than five centuries after he wrote. Several centuries were to pass before Antiochus Epiphanes would plunder the city of Jerusalem and profane the temple. So Daniel is told to "shut up the words and seal the book; even to the time of the end" (Daniel 12:4) and nearly three centuries after his death, the Maccabees found great comfort in his prophetic words. John, on the other hand, who wrote the Book of Revelation, was expressly told not to seal "the sayings of the prophecy of this book for the time is at hand" (Revelation 22:10). This surely would indicate that the events covered in his prophecy are not confined to the "week" of the Great Tribulation which has not arrived yet, even though nineteen centuries have come and gone since John wrote. A far better interpretation is found when we apply the truths as they relate to the continuing conflict between Satan and the Lord Jesus as Christ brings all enemies under His feet destroying the final enemy, death, at His coming.

6. Did Jesus "anoint the most Holy"? The New Testament answers this with an unqualified affirmative in the most explicit language. I am amazed to find Bible teachers who, like Dr. Gabelein, say, "It has nothing to do with Him [our Lord] but it is the anointing of the Holy of Holies in another temple which will stand in the midst of Jerusalem." * Only a mind that has already been made up to accept the view that the seventy weeks are not consecutive but include the entire Church Age can ignore or misread the clear statement found in Hebrews 9. The ordinances and worldly sanctuary are described (Hebrews 9:1-5); the imperfection of the ministry in the worldly sanctuary by the priests is pointed out (Hebrews 9:6-10); and then, in contrast, the perfect ministry of Christ in the heavenly sanctuary is declared (Hebrews 9:11,12).

> But Christ being come an high priest of good things to come, by a greater and more perfect tabernacle, not made with hands, that is to say, not of this building, neither by the blood of goats and calves, but by his own blood He entered once into the Holy place, having obtained eternal redemption for us (Hebrews 9:11,12).

There is no question but what our Lord did enter in with the blood of His own sacrifice to anoint the Holy of Holies in heaven and by His death He rent the veil from top to bottom that had kept all others except the High Priest out of that holy place.

> Having therefore, brethren, boldness to enter into the holiest by the blood of Jesus, by a new and living way

---

* A.C. Gabelein, *The Prophet Daniel*, p. 133.

which He hath consecrated for us through the veil, that is to say, His flesh; and having an High Priest over the house of God, let us draw near with a true heart ... (Hebrews 10:19-22a).

This was accomplished as a part of the destiny of God's people within the seventy-week period of 490 years and surely could not have a greater fulfillment in any earthly temple made with human hands.

SUMMARY

To summarize our discussion of this portion of God's prophetic message given to Daniel, I would say that there is no reason to doubt that Jesus accomplished these things at the time of His first coming. Scripture is plain and conclusive in pointing to Him and His work as the focal point of Old Testament prophecy. It is dangerous to change the obvious meaning of the words of Scripture from seventy sevens to sixty-nine plus more than 19 centuries plus one week in order to fit them into one's theory. The focal point of this prophecy is Messiah's coming and the destiny of Daniel's people was the fulfillment of God's plan to bring blessing to all the world through the Seed of Abraham. It would be strange indeed if the coming of Messiah would have nothing to do with the accomplishment of what is foretold during the 490-year period of Israel's destiny. But I believe that I have shown enough evidence from the New Testament to prove that His coming did bring about the full accomplishment of this great prophetic passage. Now we are ready to proceed with the rest of this prophecy.

Daniel 9:25-27

Know, therefore, and understand, that from the going forth of the commandment to restore and to build Jerusalem, unto the Messiah, the Prince, shall be seven weeks and threescore and two weeks: the street shall be built again, and the wall, even in troublous times. And after threescore and two weeks shall Messiah be cut off, but not for himself: and the people of the prince that shall come shall destroy the city and the sanctuary: and the end thereof shall be with a flood, and unto the end of the war desolations are determined. And he shall confirm the covenant with many for one week: and in the midst of the week he shall cause the sacrifice and the oblation to cease, and for the overspreading of abominations he shall make it desolate, even until the consummation, and that determined shall be poured upon the desolate.

Having shown what will be accomplished in the period of seventy weeks, God's messenger reveals to Daniel that there will be three divisions of this period: (1) seven weeks, during which the wall and street of Jerusalem would be built up; (2) sixty-two more weeks to the coming of the Messiah Prince; (3) one week, when He confirms a covenant with many and causes the oblation and sacrifice to cease in the midst of the week. The interpretation of this last week, the seventieth, and who confirms a covenant is most crucial in understanding much of New Testament prophecy. Pre-millennialists in general believe that the week is the week of tribulation which begins after the present church age is concluded by the rapture and that it is the Anti-Christ who confirms the covenant with Israel. Many others believe that the seventieth week followed immediately after the sixty-nine weeks and that the Messiah Himself confirms the covenant.

We shall consider this carefully, but first we must determine when this 490-year period commenced—"From the going forth of the commandment to build and restore Jerusalem." There would be no question if we could find one decree given by a Persian monarch that specifically commands that Jerusalem should be restored and built. Cyrus issued a decree which is recorded in Ezra 1:1-4 that the Jews should return and build God a house in Jerusalem, but this was given in 536 B.C. and does not mention restoring and rebuilding the city. Nehemiah, about 80 years later, received permission to go to Jerusalem from King Ahasueras in the twentieth year of his reign, 444 B.C., but there is no decree recorded, only letters which he requested that gave him authority to receive help.

SIR ROBERT ANDERSON

In the book, *The Coming Prince*, by Sir Robert Anderson, we find a detailed study of this subject. He presents a case in which he finds it exactly 483 years (sixty-nine weeks of years) from Nehemiah's departure to Jerusalem to the day of Jesus' triumphal entry. But the triumphal entry was not the beginning of Messiah's ministry. He was publicly acknowledged as "the Lamb of God that taketh away the sin of the world" by His forerunner, John the Baptist, when His ministry began, 3½ years earlier (John 1:36). Also, as recorded in John 2:13-17, on the first passover of His public ministry, Jesus came suddenly to His temple, cleansing it in fulfillment of Malachi 3:1:

> Behold, I will send my messenger, and he shall prepare the way before me: and the Lord, whom ye seek, shall suddenly come to His temple, even the messenger of the covenant, whom ye delight in: behold, He shall come, saith the Lord of hosts.

And Psalm 69:9: "The zeal of thine house hath eaten me up." Just because Sir Robert Anderson can make the 483 years terminate with the triumphal entry of Jesus into Jerusalem by using lunar years, gives no reason to overlook the fact that Israel's Messiah had come in 26 A.D. and had been ministering to Israel for 3½ years. Another serious problem that Anderson faces is that of the seventieth week, which he holds is yet to be fulfilled. He uses the principle that at certain times of punishment "their [Israel's] national existence as Jehovah's people was in abeyance," and consequently time does not count during such periods. But why should the clock stop running before Jesus sealed the covenant of promise with the house of Israel when He suffered and died on Calvary? Judgment and slavery did not really fall upon the nation for some forty years (70 A.D.) so why are these years not counted? And why should the supposed covenant between Anti-Christ and Israel (which is still thought to be a future event) start the "time-clock" so that the seventieth week is to be counted from that point on? Israel has now been back in the land for over thirty years and has not been in servitude to any nation, but still no one has claimed that the seventieth week determined upon Daniel's people has begun. Surely, it is straining the reasonable interpretation of Scripture to put 1900 plus years between the triumphal entry of Jesus into Jerusalem and the beginning of the seventieth week, and it ignores completely the primary mission of the Messiah, God's Son, which was to bring salvation to all who will believe.

DECREE IN EZRA 7

Finally, there is no decree written in the Scriptures in Nehemiah commanding the restoration and rebuilding of Jerusalem that would help us establish the year 444 B.C. as the date of the beginning of the 490-year period of prophecy. In the 20th year of King Ahasueras, Nehemiah heard that the captives returned to Jerusalem were "in great affliction and reproach: the wall of Jerusalem also is broken down and the gates thereof are burned with fire." Evidently he had expected better conditions for those who had returned to Jerusalem with Ezra by royal edict thirteen years earlier, in the seventh year of Ahasueras. After mourning and fasting and praying, he determined to do something about it and with the King's permission and letters to the governors and to Asaph, keeper of the King's forests, he went to Jerusalem and led the people in rebuilding the wall of the city.

There is, however, a decree quoted at length in Ezra 7:11-26 issued in the seventh year of the reign of the same King Ahasueras which commands that all they of the people of Israel in his realm who by their own free will wish to return to Jerusalem may go. God had promised that a second time He would bring the Jewish captives back to their land and He was faithful to that promise through King Ahasueras. This decree was issued in 457 B.C. and undoubtedly included the rebuilding of Jerusalem, for in the decree we read

> And whatsoever shall seem good to thee and to thy brethren to do with the rest of the silver and the gold, that do after the will of your God (Ezra 7:18).

In the prayer and confession of Ezra recorded in chapter 9, we read these words,

> for we were bondmen yet our God hath not forsaken us

in our bondage but hath extended mercy unto us in the sight of the kings of Persia to give us a reviving, to set up the house of God, and to repair the desolations thereof and to give us a wall in Judah and in Jerusalem (Ezra 9:9).

Evidently the decree of Artaxerxes in 457 B.C. had ordered the repair of the desolations and the wall of Jerusalem and this was what distressed Nehemiah 13 years later when he heard that the city and the walls were still broken down. This then sets the correct date of 457 B.C. to begin the seventy-week period of Daniel's prophecy, especially since the decree is fully written into the Scripture.

EXACT FULFILLMENT

Now counting 483 years from 457 B.C., we come to 26 A.D. which is the year when Jesus was pointed out as the Lamb of God by John the Baptist and began His ministry. Thus the prophecy that the street and the wall shall be built again during troublous times which lasted for seven weeks of years (49 years) was fulfilled and sixty-two more weeks of years (434 years) brings us to the beginning of Messiah's ministry, 26 A.D., which lasted for 3½ years. The prophecy also states that Messiah will be cut off after the 69 weeks "but not for himself" (also translated "and shall have nothing") and then as though in a parenthesis goes on to foretell the destruction of Jerusalem by the people of the prince that shall come which occurred when the Roman army, under the command of Titus, besieged and captured Jerusalem in 70 A.D. This is accepted so generally that there is no need for further discussion.

Certainly the most important question is whether this is where the prophecy leaves the Messiah, "cut off" and having nothing, or is He the one who confirms the covenant for one week with many, and in the midst of the week, causes the oblation and sacrifice to cease? The word "he" in verse 27 may refer either to Messiah the Prince or to the Prince, whose people would destroy Jerusalem, and it is extremely important to decide correctly which Prince is meant. The premillennial view of prophecy takes this to refer to the Prince who shall come, speculating that he is the Anti-Christ who shall come out of the revived Roman empire and that he will make a covenant with Israel guaranteeing her security for one week. However, the prophecy says that the covenant will be confirmed for one week "with many"; it does not say "with Israel." Some suggest that this covenant is the covenant of death mentioned in Isaiah 28:15,18, but a careful reading of that chapter makes it plain that it has nothing to do with Daniel's prophecy or with a future tribulation period. In fact, God's answer to Jerusalem's rulers is given in Isaiah 28:16 where Isaiah says,

> Therefore, thus saith the Lord God, Behold I lay in Zion for a foundation a stone, a tried stone, a precious corner stone, a sure foundation; he that believeth shall not make haste.

That foundation stone was laid 19 centuries ago according to the New Testament Scripture (I Peter 2:8) and proves that Jesus and faith in Him is the only answer for sinners who are all under the covenant of death.

According to the premillennial teaching, in the midst of the week the Anti-Christ breaks the covenant, stopping the Jewish sacrifices, and setting himself up as God in the rebuilt temple in Jerusalem. There is great suffering (the time of Jacob's trouble) for Israel, but at the end of the 3½ years Jesus delivers His people at His coming to earth and begins the millennium. Now most of this is not in the actual prophecy given to Daniel and has to be supplemented from other Scriptures, which are assumed to refer to this seventieth week. So read again verse 27:

> And he shall confirm the covenant with many for one week: and in the midst of the week he shall cause the sacrifice and oblation to cease, and for the overspreading of abominations he shall make it desolate even until the consummation and that determined shall be poured upon the desolate.

All that is said here is that the prince shall confirm the covenant with many for one week and in the midst of the week cause the sacrifice and oblation to cease. This obviously is the last week of the seventy and the normal interpretation of the words would be to take them as following immediately on the 69th week when Messiah has come. How then shall we interpret this important prophecy? Jeremiah had prophesied not only the return of the captives after seventy years, but also the establishment of a New Covenant replacing the Old Mosaic Covenant with Israel (Jeremiah 31:31-34). This New Covenant confirmed by Jesus with Israel was the fulfillment of God's promise to Abraham through the Seed and the consummation of Israel's destiny as a nation. Isn't it an amazing fulfillment of this prophecy that our Lord's ministry, preparing for the New Covenant in Israel, lasted 3½ years, that in the midst of the week He was sacrificed on Calvary, causing Israel's temple ritual of sacrifice and oblation to cease and then, after His resurrection, He continued through His disciples for 3½ years to confirm the covenant, not with the nation which rejected it, but with the many who believed. It is through this covenant confirmed by the blood of Jesus that Israel fulfilled her destiny, not through the unbelieving physical descendants of Abraham, but through the believing remnant of whom Jesus was the true Seed. For the nation that refused her King there was only the promise of the destruction of the sanctuary and the city and desolation. The awful words of Jesus come to mind which He spoke to the leaders of Israel, "Behold, your house is left unto you desolate" (Matthew 23:38). It would seem that this would mark the end of Israel as a nation and the question is asked in the Scriptures, "Hath God cast away His people?" How important it is for us to know what the answer is from the Scripture and to believe what God has in store for Israel. We turn then to consider Israel under the New Covenant.

CHAPTER IX

Israel's New Covenant In Christ

ISRAEL HAD EXISTED as a nation in covenant relationship with God ever since the day when they were encamped at Mt. Sinai and the Lord challenged them to accept His commandments and obey His voice. In Exodus 19:3-8, we have the record:

> And Moses went up unto God and the Lord called unto him out of the mountain, saying, Thus shalt thou say to the house of Jacob and tell the children of Israel; ye have seen what I did with the Egyptians, and how I bare you on eagle's wings and brought you unto myself. Now, therefore, if ye will obey my voice indeed, and keep my covenant, then ye shall be a peculiar treasure unto me above all people; for all the earth is mine: and ye shall be unto me a kingdom of priests and an holy nation. These are the words which thou shalt speak unto the children of Israel. And Moses came and called for the elders of the people and laid before their faces all these words which

the Lord commanded him. And all the people answered together and said, All that the Lord hath spoken we will do. And Moses returned the words of the people unto the Lord.

Then God laid upon that nation the commandments and laws that were necessary for the ordering of their life. He prescribed for them a tabernacle with a ritual of sacrifices, feasts and worship performed by priests, culminating each year in the Day of Atonement, the only day in the year when the High Priest could go in to the Holy of Holies with the blood of the sacrifice to sprinkle the mercy seat of the Ark of the Covenant. The Old Covenant was made with the nation on the principle, "do this and thou shalt live." But as we saw in an earlier chapter, the law could not bring salvation because sinful flesh could not perfectly keep the law. If a person breaks God's law at one point he is guilty as a law-breaker and is under the condemnation of death unless delivered by Christ the Saviour. It is very important in understanding God's covenant relationship with the nation of Israel that we recognize this complete failure of the Old Mosaic Covenant and the absolute necessity of the establishment of the New Covenant, confirmed by Christ Jesus and sealed with His precious blood.

In order to understand the differences between the Old and the New Covenants which we are discussing, it will be clearer if we place in contrast some of the plain provisions of each.

THE OLD MOSAIC COVENANT	**THE NEW COVENANT IN CHRIST**

Mediated through Moses, God's servant; Moses was faithful in God's house. Blessings were conditional upon obedience to God's laws:
    a. possession of the land
    b. material prosperity
    c. victory over enemies
	Mediated by Jesus, God's Son; Jesus was faithful over His own house. The promise was in Christ—guaranteed by God's oath:
	    a. a better heavenly country
	    b. abundant life with spiritual blessings
	    c. made more than conquerors through Christ.

The Mosaic Covenant was everlasting in the sense of perpetual, until superceded through your generations.	The New Covenant is everlasting in the full sense of eternal.
The Law required circumcision of the flesh.	The New Covenant requires circumcision of the heart.
The Law was the ministration of condemnation and death.	The New Covenant is God's gift of eternal life in Jesus Christ.
The Law was temporary until the Seed should come.	The New Covenant makes us subjects by faith in an everlasting Kingdom.
The Law was a shadow of coming reality.	The New Covenant is the reality through the finished work of Christ.
The Law failed through the weakness of the flesh.	The New Covenant accomplished God's goal by His grace and power.
The Law was given to Israel as a nation.	The New Covenant is made with believing Israel for all believers.
The Law required many sacrifices.	The New Covenant was established by one perfect sacrifice— the Lamb of God.
The Law provided a mortal priesthood through successive generations.	The New Covenant presents the eternal perfect High Priest, Jesus Christ.
The Law provided a temple built by human hands.	The New Covenant makes us into a living temple, Christ the chief cornerstone.
Under the Law, salvation was in Israel and ritual observances were required.	Under the New Covenant, salvation is only through faith in Jesus Christ.
The Law says, "This do and thou shalt live"—result is failure.	The New Covenant says, "Believe receive life and do His will"— our failure is already forgiven in Christ.

Let us ask then the question, "Under what covenant does Israel exist as a nation today in its relation to God?" I firmly believe that the only answer one can give that is in accord with the Scriptures is that they are under the covenant made with Israel when Jesus died and rose again. Of course, I recognize that this is in conflict with the popular teaching that Israel has been set aside during the church age and, after Christ comes to rapture the church, God will begin again to deal with Israel nationally. So it is necessary to consider this teaching and point out the errors in interpretation which are involved.

1. It is commonly taught by dispensationalists and pre-millennialists that the Old Testament prophecies of a glorious kingdom under a Davidic king must be interpreted literally as a kingdom established in peace and security in the land with the Messiah sitting upon the literal throne of David, ruling over Israel. The rejection of Jesus as their king is excused by these teachers because, they say, the Jews rightly expected such a king to reign in fulfillment of prophecy and Jesus was not that kind of king. But how wrong this is! Who has determined that the words of prophecy must always be interpreted with a literal meaning? Why don't we listen to the words of Jesus who said so plainly, "My kingdom is not of this world" and refused to let the people crown Him? Why can't we hear Him say, "The kingdom shall be taken from you and given to a nation bringing forth the fruits thereof"? He Himself does not say that the kingdom will be restored to Israel but says, "Fear not, little flock, for it is the Father's good pleasure to give you the Kingdom." When James and John wanted the important seats on His right and left when He established His kingdom, Jesus immediately explains to the disciples that in His kingdom, ambition is not for prominent position but for greatness in humble service.

Take just one of many Old Testament prophecies to see the nature of the kingdom promised to Israel. Zechariah 9:9 gives us very familiar words,

Rejoice greatly O daughter of Zion; shout, O daughter of Jerusalem: behold, thy King cometh unto thee; He is

just and having salvation: lowly and riding upon an ass
and upon a colt the foal of an ass.

These were wonderfully fulfilled literally by the triumphal
entry of our Lord into Jerusalem. But don't stop there—the
prophet has more to say in verse 10:

And I will cut off the chariot from Ephraim and the
horse from Jerusalem and the battle bow shall be cut
off: and He shall speak peace unto the heathen: and His
dominion shall be from sea even to sea and from the
river even to the ends of the earth.

Was this second part of the prophecy fulfilled by the King's
coming or do we have to arbitrarily insert 1900 years
between verse 9 and 10? Certainly the chariot horse and
battle bow were cut off from Ephraim and Jerusalem in 70
A.D. Certainly the King spoke peace to the heathen (Ephesians 2:14-17). Are we to deny that Jesus brought peace to the
heathen because He didn't set up His throne in Jerusalem
and have His ambassadors sign peace treaties with the
nations? He made peace through the blood of His cross and
He gives to human hearts who trust Him a peace that the
world cannot give or take away. Isn't this the kind of peace
Zechariah was foretelling in chapter 9:10?

Furthermore, Jesus did not come to the world to be an
earthly king. When His birth was announced to the
shepherds by the angel he said, "For unto you is born this
day in the city of David a Saviour which is Christ the Lord."
A Saviour first—the glory of the King of Kings would follow
His sufferings. In His own words He declares the purpose of
His coming: "The Son of Man is come to seek and to save that
which was lost" (Luke 19:10). "Even as the Son of man came
not to be ministered unto, but to minister and to give His life
a ransom for many" (Matthew 20:28). "I am the good
shepherd: the good shepherd giveth His life for the sheep"
(John 10:11). "Then He said unto them, O fools and slow of
heart to believe all that the prophets have spoken. Ought not
Christ to have suffered these things and to enter into His
glory?" (Luke 24:25,26).

2. It is commonly taught by dispensationalists and pre-
millennialists that the church is a "parenthesis" in God's

program with Israel and that it is a Gentile church. How anyone can hold such a view in the light of the clear teaching of Scripture is difficult to understand. In Ephesians 2:12-22, we have clear teaching on this subject.

> That at that time ye were without Christ, being aliens from the commonwealth of Israel, and strangers from the covenants of promise, having no hope, and without God in the world. But now in Christ Jesus ye who sometimes were far off are made nigh by the blood of Christ. For He is our peace, who hath made both one, and hath broken down the middle wall of partition between us; having abolished in His flesh the enmity, even the law of commandments contained in ordinances; for to make in Himself of twain one new man, so making peace; And that He might reconcile both unto God in one body by the cross, having slain the enmity thereby: and came and preached peace to you which are afar off, and to them that are nigh. For through Him we both have access by one Spirit unto the Father. Now therefore ye are no more strangers and foreigners, but fellow citizens with the saints, and of the household of God; and are built upon the foundation of the apostles and prophets, Jesus Christ Himself being the chief cornerstone; in whom all the building, fitly framed together, groweth unto an holy temple in the Lord; In whom ye also are builded together for an habitation of God through the Spirit.

Note that after describing the Gentiles as "without Christ, being aliens from the commonwealth of Israel and strangers from the covenants of promise, having no hope and without God in the world" (vs. 12), Jesus Christ, by His blood, made it possible for them to come near (vs. 13). Christ is our peace. He has made Jew and Gentile one, having broken down the middle wall that separated the two (vs. 14). He did this by suffering in His flesh, satisfying the demands of the law and thus abolishing the "law of commandments contained in ordinances." His purpose was to make of Jew and Gentile "one new man, so making peace" (vs. 15). There is no indication that God wishes to keep the Jew separate from the Gentile; rather He would like to reconcile both Jew and Gentile unto Himself in one body by the cross since He has slain the enmity between them by dying on that cross (vs. 16). However, He has kept unbelieving Israel under judgment of partial blindness through nineteen centuries for His purpose of grace as we shall see in our study of Romans, chapter 11. Certainly if St. Paul could wish himself accursed from Christ if that would mean salvation for the Jews, his kinsmen according to the flesh, how it must grieve the heart of God for Israel to remain a stubborn and rebellious people except for the small remnant who believe in Jesus their Messiah.

Far from being a Gentile church, the fact is that the New Covenant was confirmed with Israel by the Saviour; the first members of the church were all Jews; for 3½ years the gospel was preached only to Jews; and when the nation had had its full opportunity to receive her Messiah and had not only refused to believe but began to persecute all who did believe, then the door was opened wide to include the Gentiles and they became not just members of the church but fellow citizens with the saints (Jews) and of the household of God (which had been Israel). It was not God's wish to create a Gentile church and He has always kept a remnant of Jewish believers in the "body" or "bride" of Christ by His election (Romans 11:5).

The church is not a Gentile church nor is it merely a parenthesis in God's overall program with Israel. The church is the household of God including true believers of all of human history. If we define the true church or "called out ones" as the body of those who believe in God through the Messiah, Jesus Christ, then there was a church in Israel during the Old Testament dispensation for there was a body of true believers who had faith in the coming Messiah and kept that faith alive from the days of Abraham to the time of Christ. The present church is built upon the foundation of the apostles and prophets, Jesus Christ Himself being the Chief Cornerstone.

THE CHURCH IN THE OLD TESTAMENT

After the revelation of God in Jesus Christ and the gift of the Holy Spirit, the church took on a different form from what it had been for fifteen centuries within the commonwealth of Israel. No longer were the people of God under bondage to the law and ordinances of Judaism. They were saved by faith without the law, both Jews and Gentiles (Acts 15:10,11) and the Saviour gave His Holy Spirit to abide in the hearts of all who would receive Him. It was under a different dispensation of God's economy but the church was built upon the foundation of the apostles and prophets and you cannot separate the building from its foundation. Did not Jesus say concerning the faith of the centurion, whose servant He healed:

> Verily I say unto you, I have not found so great faith, no, not in Israel. And I say unto you, that many shall come from the east and west and sit down with Abraham, and Isaac, and Jacob in the kingdom of heaven. But the children of the kingdom shall be cast out into outer darkness...(Matthew 8:10b-12a).

How could Jesus more plainly say that faith is the basis of anyone's entrance into the kingdom of heaven and that many Gentiles would by faith enjoy a blessed union with the fathers of Israel while many Jews, children of the kingdom, would be excluded because they refused to believe? Thank God, there will not be two separate groups in heaven, Jews and Gentiles, but there will be "one flock and one shepherd" including all believers in one family of God the Father.

3. Another error commonly taught is that the church is not found in the Old Testament Scriptures. In a limited sense, it is possible to make such an affirmation, for technically it is true that no specific prophecy foretells in so many words an exact description of the institutional church. However, just because such literal prophecies cannot be found in the writings of the prophets, for one to say that "the church is not in the Old Testament" is a serious error because he fails to recognize that the New Covenant, with the blessings flowing from that covenant for both Jew and Gentile on a worldwide basis, is the primary subject of much of Old Testament prophecy. Is not the "rock," which is the foundation upon which Jesus says He will build His church, the focal point of all of prophecy? When Jesus walked with the two disciples on the road to Emmaus after His resurrection, He chided them for their unbelief and "beginning at Moses and all the prophets He expounded unto them in all the

scriptures the things concerning Himself." What was He telling them about Himself? Only those things that had to do with Israel after His Second Coming? Or did He speak of the work He had accomplished by His death and resurrection as the hope of the world for salvation and of the forgiveness and righteousness that were to be proclaimed to all the world?

When the apostle Paul quotes the words of Isaiah 64:4, "Eye hath not seen nor ear heard neither have entered into the heart of man the things which God hath prepared for them that love Him" (I Corinthians 2:9); he adds, "...but God hath revealed them unto us by His Spirit" (I Corinthians 2:10a). Isaiah prophesied of "things which God had prepared" for believers and Paul says he was prophesying of things revealed to us who are in the church. Again, Paul is surely referring to the church when he says, "For whatsoever things were written aforetime were written for our learning, that we through patience and comfort of the scriptures might have hope" (Romans 15:4). He quotes four times from the Old Testament Scriptures to prove that our Lord's work of confirming the promises made unto the fathers should give the Gentiles cause for glorifying God (Romans 15:9-12). There can be no doubt but that he is speaking of Gentiles in the church now. Once more in this same chapter (Romans 15) in verse 21, Paul quotes an Old Testament Scripture and applies it to the preaching of the gospel in the church age (Romans 15:21). "But as it is written, to whom He was not spoken of, they shall see: and they that have not heard shall understand" (quoted from Isaiah 52:15).

In Galatians 3:8, we read,

And the scripture foreseeing that God would justify the heathen through faith preached before the gospel unto Abraham saying, In thee shall all nations be blessed.

Clearly Paul is saying that the same gospel which he was preaching, the gospel of salvation by faith, was really the gospel preached to Abraham when he was given the promise of the Seed that would bless the world and he believed.

Listen once more to the Apostle Paul in the great doxology with which he closes his letter to the Romans:

Now to Him that is of power to establish you according to my gospel and the preaching of Jesus Christ, according to the revelation of the mystery, which was kept secret since the world began, but is now made manifest and by the scriptures of the prophets according to the commandment of the everlasting God, made known to all nations for the obedience of faith (Romans 16:25,26).

Here he identifies his preaching of the gospel with the revelation of the mystery which was kept hidden since the world began. But he does not say that his preaching or the revealed mystery which he now was preaching had nothing to do with the Old Testament Scriptures or prophets, but that it is now "made manifest and by the scriptures of the prophets...made known to all nations." How can teachers of the Bible say that the church which resulted from this preaching of the now-revealed "mystery" was not in the Old Testament when this Scripture so plainly says that it was made known "by the scriptures of the prophets"?

Most convincing is the passage in I Peter 1:10-12. The apostle, speaking of the salvation we have in Christ, says:

Of which salvation the prophets have inquired and searched diligently, who prophesied of the grace that should come unto you: searching what, or what manner of time the Spirit of Christ which was in them did signify, when it testified beforehand the sufferings of Christ and the glory that should follow. Unto whom it was revealed that not unto themselves but unto us they did minister the things which are now reported unto you by them that have preached the gospel unto you with the Holy Ghost sent down from heaven; which things the angels desire to look into.

When Scripture plainly says that the prophets "prophesied of the grace which should come unto you" and he can only mean you who are in Christ, members of His church, I fail to understand how a Bible teacher can say that the church is not in the Old Testament. Those prophets ministered "not unto themselves but unto us," the members of the body of Christ and we are the church.

There are many other New Testament quotations that prove that Old Testament prophecy was concerned with the redeeming and saving work of our Lord Jesus during this church age, but we cannot consider them all in the space we have. I hope enough has been included to show that the church age, during which by the Lord's command, the gospel of salvation is to be preached in all the world to every creature, was very much in the mind of God when He spoke through the Old Testament prophets. It is a tragic mistake to refer all the Old Testament Scriptures to the nation of Israel, anticipating a literal fulfillment of supposed promises of still future glory and world domination for the natural seed of Abraham.

4. Another serious error in this teaching is that Israel will still be under the covenant of law after the close of the church age and on through the tribulation period. One writer says:

> When this age [the age of the law] is resumed—the Jewish age has been cut short as we noted in Daniel's prophecy—judgment will follow upon Israel in that time known as the 'time of Jacob's trouble.'

And he says also that

> In the end of this dispensation of the law there will be tokens of grace also in the ministry of the tribulation remnant and God's care for them, as well as the multitude saved out of the nations upon the earth.*

Here the author is saying that the age or dispensation of law will be resumed and will be in effect when the tribulation occurs and a multitude is being saved. This is in conflict with the clear teaching of the New Testament, especially in the 8th chapter of Hebrews, verses 6-13. The writer of Hebrews is concerned to show to Christians of Jewish background the superiority of the "better" covenant made upon better promises with a better sacrifice offered by a better High Priest, our Lord Jesus Christ. He describes the tabernacle made with men's hands, its furnishings, its animal sacrifices, its mortal priesthood, and says this is but a shadow of the reality in Jesus, the Great High Priest. Now, speaking of the two covenants, here he says,

> For if that first covenant had been faultless, then should no place have been sought for the second. For finding fault with them, He saith, Behold the days come, saith

---

*Fineberg, *Premillennialism and Amillennialism*, p. 83.

the Lord, when I will make a new covenant with the house of Israel and with the house of Judah: Not according to the covenant that I made with their fathers in the day when I took them by the hand to lead them out of the land of Egypt; because they continued not in my covenant and I regarded them not, saith the Lord. For this is the covenant that I will make with the house of Israel after those days, saith the Lord; I will put my laws into their mind and write them in their hearts; and I will be to them a God and they shall be my people: and they shall not teach every man his neighbor and every man his brother, saying, Know the Lord: for all shall know me, from the least to the greatest. For I will be merciful to their unrighteousness, and their sins and their iniquities will I remember no more. In that he saith, a new covenant, he hath made the first old. Now that which decayeth and waxeth old is ready to vanish away (Hebrews 8:7-13).

Within a few years, Jerusalem was taken by the Romans, the temple destroyed, the priesthood and sacrifices ended, most of the people put to death, the survivors scattered, and the existence of Israel as a nation ceased. Truly the Old Covenant was done away. Was it Rome that had caused it to vanish? No. It was Christ who had fulfilled the law and had replaced it with the New Covenant in His precious blood, which in reality was the original covenant of promise "that was confirmed before of God in Christ" to Abraham (Galatians 3:17). Some may try to argue that the New Covenant, promised in Jeremiah 31:31ff was not made with Israel at our Lord's first coming, but will be at His second coming. This not only contradicts the fact of history that the Jews were the only ones with whom the New Covenant was first confirmed, but also would leave Israel with no covenant during these centuries. No one would argue that Jews have been converted and accepted under the New Covenant in Christ. Why would God put those Jews who believe under the New Covenant and leave the rest under the Old Mosaic Covenant? Scripture says that the law failed, it could not give life to sinners, "what the law could not do in that it was weak through the flesh, God sending His own Son in the likeness of sinful flesh and for sin, condemned sin in the flesh" (Romans 8:4). We conclude then that Israel is no longer under the law, and we do not believe that God will ever place Israel or anyone else under the law again when He already once and for all has provided His answer to the law in the sacrifice of His Only Begotten Son.

5. Another error in this kind of teaching is in the hope of material blessing and glory for the physical seed of Israel as a nation. This view violates the New Testament teaching that the middle wall of partition was torn down through Jesus' sufferings in the flesh (Ephesians 2:15). He abolished the enmity between Jew and Gentile, even the law of commandments, the law that had kept the Jew a distinct and separate people and He did this in order to make them both one, in one body through His cross so making peace. Again, we ask when at such a price as the suffering of His Son on Calvary God erased the distinction between Jew and Gentile and desires that they all shall be one in Him, is it conceivable that He will raise the barrier once more and share His glory with the physical seed of Abraham in an earthly Kingdom? The spirit of humility shown by John the Baptist when he said of Jesus, "He must increase but I must decrease" (John 3:30) is certainly far more appropriate to Christ's Kingdom than the ambition to share His glory ruling the world for a thousand years with a rod of iron.

UNDER WHICH COVENANT?

Having considered some of the errors that we find commonly taught concerning Israel's present covenant relation with God, we are now ready to answer the original question in this chapter: Under what covenant does Israel exist as a nation today in its relation to God? The answer of Scripture is plain: they are under the New Covenant sealed by the blood of Christ, redeemed from the bondage and curse of the law and made heirs of salvation if only they will believe. The Old Covenant was abolished when its demands were fulfilled by the promised Seed of Abraham and the Covenant of Promise, confirmed with God's oath to Abraham 430 years before the Mosaic Covenant of law was given, was now effective for the believing Jew first and also for the believing Gentile. This New Covenant of Promise did not need to be ratified and accepted by Israel as a nation before it could be effective. This covenant was based on the finished work of the Saviour Messiah and not upon the conditional promise of obedience by the people or nation. This covenant proclaimed remission of sins to all who believe and everlasting righteousness and adoption as children of God through faith in the atoning sacrifice and victorious resurrection of Jesus. Even though the nation refused to have the King and cried out, "Crucify Him, crucify Him," that could not nullify the Promised Covenant. This is why Peter could stand before the great crowd that gathered on the Day of Pentecost and declare, "Therefore, let all the House of Israel know assuredly that God hath made that same Jesus, whom ye have crucified, both Lord and Christ" (Acts 2:36). He went on to say to them,

> Repent and be baptized everyone of you in the name of Jesus Christ for the remission of sins and ye shall receive the gift of the Holy Ghost. For the promise is unto you and to your children and to all that are afar off even as many as the Lord Our God shall call (Acts 2:38).

This was the New Covenant and was proclaimed to all who would hear, even to those who crucified the Lord of Glory. How amazing is God's grace!

Is there any doubt in your mind that Israel was included in the New Covenant of Promise which replaced the Old Covenant? Then listen once more to Peter in his second recorded sermon as he spoke to the people after healing the lame man at the Beautiful Gate of the temple.

> Ye are the children of the prophets and of the covenant which God made with our fathers, saying unto Abraham, 'And in thy Seed shall all the kindreds of the earth be blessed.' Unto you first God having raised up His Son Jesus, sent Him to bless you, in turning away everyone of you from his iniquities (Acts 3:25,26).

Those who repented and believed found forgiveness and righteousness and eternal salvation through their faith in the risen Messiah, and if all the Jews had repented, I believe there was enough grace to include all. But the sad story tells of unbelief which resulted in hardened hearts and culminated in mad hatred of the very Name of Jesus and persecution of those who believed in or proclaimed that Name.

At some point the judgment of "blindness in part" was placed upon the nation (Romans 11:25) and while the Spirit still convicted their hearts of sin, only a relatively few Jews received the Messiah. This is the same blindness spoken of by Isaiah the prophet who prophesied before the conquest and captivity of the Northern Kingdom of Israel around 720 B.C.:

> And He said, Go and tell this people, Hear ye indeed, but understand not: and see ye indeed but perceive not. Make the heart of this people fat and make their ears heavy, and shut their eyes; lest they see with their eyes, and hear with their ears and understand with their heart and convert and be healed (Isaiah 6:9,10).

Jesus quotes these words of Isaiah and applies them to the people of His day who refused to really hear His words and see His miracles and understand who He was. Paul, after he preached the message of salvation in Rome as a prisoner for Christ's sake, quotes the same prophetic words concerning the Jews who refused the gospel of Jesus Christ and said, "Be it known therefore unto you, that the salvation of God is sent unto the Gentiles and they will hear it" (Acts 28:28).

Then within the span of that first generation, the Roman armies conquered Jerusalem and Jesus' awful words were fulfilled,

> That upon you may come all the righteous blood shed upon the earth from the blood of righteous Abel unto the blood of Zacharias son of Barachias, whom ye slew between the temple and the altar. Verily I say unto you, All these things shall come upon this generation. Behold your house is left unto you desolate (Matthew 23:35,36,38).

RESTORATION OF ISRAEL TODAY

If Israel does not have a covenant as a separate nation with God and exists now under the Abrahamic Covenant of Promise in the true Seed, Jesus the Messiah, how is it that today she again is a nation and God has preserved a scattered people for so many centuries with a unique identity? In answer I would say: (1) I believe that God's desire for Israel through these centuries has been that they would believe on His Son and be part of His Bride. (2) As long as they have hardened their hearts and stumbled at the cross, he has continued to leave the judgment of blindness upon them as a nation. (3) Jesus prophesied that "Jerusalem would be trodden under foot of the Gentiles until the times of the Gentiles be fulfilled" (Luke 21:24); therefore, to fulfill His words, the day has come when that city is back under the control of Israel. Truly a miracle of God's providence! (4) God has the purpose of showing the world the riches of His grace by removing the judgmental blindness, which has remained on the unbelieving and rebellious nation for over 1900 years, and by allowing most (if not all) to come to saving faith before He comes for His church for the Scripture says, "so all Israel shall be saved" (Romans 11:26a).

The wonder of God's foreknowledge and the fullness of His predictive message in the Old Testament is amazingly brought out in the great prophecy of Jeremiah 31:31-34 which I have already referred to. After announcing the confirming of a New Covenant with the house of Israel, He gives assurance of the perpetuity of the seed of Israel as a nation and prophesies that He will not cast off all the seed of Israel for all that they have done (Jeremiah 31:35-37). Why would He even consider letting the seed of Israel cease from being a nation or why should He consider casting off the seed of Israel? Because He knew how they would treat His Son. Because He knew they would not want His Son to reign over them. Because He knew they would want His Son crucified, dead and buried. So when they actually taunted Jesus and mocked and ridiculed Him as He hung on the cross, they were still included in the Covenant of Promise and God did not fail to preserve the seed and give the opportunity to believe to everyone that would hear.

CHAPTER X

God's Lament Over Israel

W HILE GOD HAS REVEALED HIMSELF as a God of infinite love and mercy, at the same time He has shown us His perfect holiness and His judgment upon all unrighteousness. It is at the cross where the Father laid the sin of the world upon His Beloved Son and accepted Him as the sacrifice, making an all-sufficient atonement for sinners, that we see most perfectly the righteousness and love of God displayed. He is a God of compassion, not willing that any should perish but that all should come to repentance. He expresses His indignation over the recurring apostasy of Israel and their oft-repeated lapses into forbidden idolatry. His indignation turns to wrath which brings severe and devastating judgment when His chosen nation continues in stubborn refusal to repent and to hear and obey His Word. But through her history, God has continued to plead with His people to be a believing people, putting their trust in Him and walking in righteousness and truth. Even after they put the Son of God upon the cross with the authority of Rome supporting their action, God still has extended His love and mercy to any of them who will believe.

In this chapter, I want you to listen to the words of God gathered from various Scripture passages as He expresses His attitudes and feelings, His yearning and longing that His people should repent and receive the love He offers, His sorrow over their sufferings which result from their rebellion, His desire that they should believe and find life in Him.

The attitudes and feelings of God for His chosen nation as expressed through Moses: Deuteronomy 7:6-11.

verse

6   For thou art an holy people unto the Lord thy God: The Lord Thy God hath chosen thee to be a special people unto Himself, above all people that are upon the face of the earth.

7   The Lord did not set His love upon you nor choose you because ye were more in number than any people; for ye were the fewest of all people:

8   But because the Lord loved you and because He would keep the oath which He had sworn unto your fathers, hath the Lord brought you out with a mighty hand and redeemed you out of the house of bondmen, from the hand of Pharoah, King of Egypt.

9   Know therefore that the Lord Thy God, He is God, the faithful God which keepeth covenant and mercy with them that love Him and keep His commandments to a thousand generations.

10   And repayeth them that hate Him to their face to destroy them: He will not be slack to him that hateth Him, He will repay him to his face.

11   Thou shalt therefore keep the commandments and the statutes and the judgments which I command thee this day, to do them.

Through Moses God expresses His indignation and disappointment over Israel's murmuring, complaining, unbelieving and stubbornly rebellious spirit during their sojourn in the wilderness.

Exodus 32:9,10

And the Lord said unto Moses, I have seen this people, and, behold, it is a stiff-necked people: Now therefore let me alone, that my wrath may wax hot against them, and that I may consume them: and I will make of thee a great nation.

Deuteronomy 9:6-8,13,14,23-24

6-8 Understand therefore that the Lord thy God giveth thee not this good land to possess it for thy righteousness for thou art a stiff-necked people. Remember and forget not how thou provokedst the Lord thy God to wrath in the wilderness: from the day that thou didst depart out of the land of Egypt until ye came unto this place, ye have been rebellious against the Lord. Also in Horeb ye provoked the Lord to wrath, so that the Lord was angry with you to have destroyed you....

13 Furthermore the Lord spake unto me saying, I have seen this people: and behold it is a stiff-necked people: Let me alone that I may destroy them and blot out their name from under heaven: and I will make of thee a nation mightier and greater than they....

23 Likewise when the Lord sent you from Kadesh-barnea saying, go up and possess the land which I have given you: then ye rebelled against the commandment of the Lord your God and ye believed Him not nor hearkened to His voice. Ye have been rebellious against the Lord from the day that I knew you.

Deuteronomy 32:18,20

18 Of the Rock that begat thee thou art unmindful, and hast forgotten God that formed thee.

20 And He said, I will hide my face from them, I will see what their end shall be: for they are a very forward generation, children in whom is no faith.

Through the prophets God pleads with Israel to repent and escape the impending judgment He has determined to bring upon them for their sins.

Hosea 11:1,3,4a

1   When Israel was a child, then I loved him and called my son out of Egypt.

3   I taught Ephraim also to go taking them by their arms; but they knew not that I healed them.

4a   I drew them with cords of a man, with bands of love.

Hosea 13:9

O Israel thou hast destroyed thyself: but in me is thine help.

Isaiah 1:2,3,4,9

2   Hear O heavens and give ear, O earth: for the Lord hath spoken. I have nourished and brought up children and they have rebelled against me.

3   The ox knoweth his owner, and the ass his master's crib: but Israel doth not know, my people doth not consider.

4   Ah sinful nation, a people laden with iniquity, a seed of evil doers, children that are corrupters: they have forsaken the Lord, they have provoked the Holy One of Israel unto anger: they have gone away backward.

9   Except the Lord of Hosts had left unto us a very small remnant we should have been as Sodom and we should have been like unto Gomorrah.

Isaiah 1:18-20

18   Come now and let us reason together, saith the Lord. Though your sins be as scarlet they shall be as white as snow; though they be red like crimson, they shall be as wool.

19   If ye be willing and obedient ye shall eat the good of the land.

20   But if ye refuse and rebel, ye shall be devoured with the sword for the mouth of the Lord hath spoken it.

Jeremiah 2:4-13

4   Hear ye the word of the Lord, O House of Jacob and all the families of the house of Israel:

5   Thus saith the Lord, What iniquity have your fathers

found in me, that they have gone far from me, and have walked after vanity and are become vain?

7 And I brought you into a plentiful country, to eat the fruit thereof and the goodness thereof: but when ye entered, ye defiled my land and made mine heritage an abomination.

9 Wherefore I will yet plead with you saith the Lord and with your children's children will I plead.

11 Hath a nation changed their gods, which are yet no gods? But my people have changed their glory for that which doth not profit.

12 Be astonished O ye heavens at this and be horribly afraid, be ye very desolate saith the Lord.

13 For my people have committed two evils; they have forsaken me, the fountain of living waters, and hewed them out cisterns, broken cisterns, that can hold no water.

Jeremiah 3:12-14

12 Go and proclaim these words toward the north and say, Return thou backsliding Israel said the Lord; and I will not cause mine anger to fall upon you; for I am merciful and I will not keep anger forever.

13 Only acknowledge thine iniquity that thou hast transgressed against the Lord Thy God...and ye have not obeyed my voice, saith the Lord.

14 Turn O backsliding children, saith the Lord; for I am married to you: and I will take you one of a city and two of a family, and I will bring you to Zion.

Jeremiah 8:18-22; 9:1

18 When I would comfort myself against sorrow, my heart is faint in me.

19 Behold the voice of the cry of the daughter of my people because of them that dwell in a far country: Is not the Lord in Zion? Is not her king in her? Why have they provoked me to anger with their graven images and with strange vanities?

20 The harvest is past and the summer is ended and we are not saved.

21 For the hurt of the daughter of my people am I hurt; I am black: astonishment hath taken hold on me.

22   Is there no balm in Gilead; is there no physician there? Why then is not the health of the daughter of my people recovered?

1   O that my head were waters and mine eyes a fountain of tears, that I might weep day and night for the slain of the daughter of my people.

Jeremiah 13:15,17

15   Hear ye and give ear: be not proud: for the Lord hath spoken.

17   But if ye will not hear it, my soul shall weep in secret places for your pride; and mine eyes shall weep sore and run down with tears because the Lord's flock is carried away captive.

Ezekiel 18:30-32

30   Therefore I will judge you, O house of Israel, every one according to his ways, saith the Lord God. Repent, and turn yourselves from all your transgressions; so iniquity shall not be your ruin.

31   Cast away from you all your transgressions, whereby ye have transgressed; and make you a new heart and a new spirit: for why will ye die, O house of Israel?

32   For I have no pleasure in the death of him that dieth saith the Lord God: wherefore turn yourselves and live ye.

God's great love for the nation that was destroying itself by rejecting their Messiah, the only Saviour, is shown by the tears of Jesus as He wept over the city of Jerusalem.

Matthew 23:37,38

37   O Jerusalem, Jerusalem, thou that killest the prophets and stonest them which are sent unto thee, how often would I have gathered thy children together even as a hen gathereth her chickens under her wings and ye would not!

38   Behold, your house is left unto you desolate.

Luke 23:28-31

28 But Jesus turning unto them said, Daughters of Jerusalem, weep not for me, but weep for yourselves and for your children.

29 For behold the days are coming, in the which they shall say, Blessed are the barren and the wombs that never bare and the paps which never gave suck.

30 Then shall they begin to say to the mountains, Fall on us; and to the hills, Cover us.

31 For if they do these things in a green tree, what shall be done in the dry?

Luke 19:41-44

41 And when He was come near, He beheld the city and wept over it.

42 Saying, If thou hadst known, even thou, at least in this thy day, the things that belong unto thy peace! but now they are hid from thine eyes.

43 For the days shall come upon thee, that thine enemies shall cast a trench about thee and compass thee round and keep thee in on every side.

44 And shall lay thee even with the ground, and thy children within thee: and they shall not leave in thee one stone upon another; because thou knewest not the time of thy visitation.

God's continued longing and yearning for Israel's salvation is expressed in the words of the Apostle Paul, who was appointed to be Christ's ambassador to the Gentiles.

Romans 10:1-3

1 Brethren, my heart's desire and prayer to God for Israel is that they might be saved.

2 For I bear them record that they have a zeal of God but not according to knowledge.

3 For they being ignorant of God's righteousness, and going about to establish their own righteousness have not submitted themselves unto the righteousness of God.

Romans 9:1-5

1 I say the truth in Christ, I lie not, my conscience also bearing witness in the Holy Ghost,

2 That I have great heaviness and continual sorrow in my heart.

3 For I could wish myself accursed from Christ for my brethren, my kinsmen according to the flesh:

4 Who are Israelites; to whom pertaineth the adoption, and the glory, and the covenants, and the giving of the law, and the service of God and the promises;

5 Whose are the fathers and of whom as concerning the flesh Christ came, who is over all, God blessed forever, Amen.

Romans 10:21

But to Israel He saith, All day long I have stretched forth my hands unto a disobedient and gainsaying people.

CHAPTER XI

Conclusion and Appeal For Prayer

As we come to the conclusion of this brief book in which I have tried to discuss God's plan of salvation through the seed of Abraham and His covenant promises and relationship with the nation of Israel, I realize that there are still many questions concerning individual prophecies and their interpretation that are unanswered. My purpose in writing has not been to furnish a question-and-answer book on Bible prophecies, but rather to discover from the Scripture and then formulate the basic principles on which God dealt with Israel through history and will deal with her in these final days before Jesus comes again. This method gives us the key to understand and interpret specific prophetic utterances or passages and we will read them in the light of the truth revealed in the Scriptures themselves. We dare not come to God's Word with a preconceived scheme and try to force the prophecies of Scripture into our mold, often doing violence to other clear teachings of the Bible. The revelation that God has given us is wonderful and perfect in the way the New Covenant in Jesus the Messiah fulfills the foreshadowing and typology which we discover in the Old Covenant. It is supremely important that we permit the writers of the New Testament, who were taught by the Lord Himself and by His Holy Spirit, to guide us into a full understanding of the prophetic message of God's Word. Let me remind you then of these basic principles which we have discovered.

1. The Promise and Eternal Covenant was given in Christ the true Seed of Abraham, and to all that are in Him, the seed of faith. Jesus, the Messiah, is the focal point of prophecy, not the natural, physical seed of Abraham.

2. The material promises to the physical seed as a nation were conditioned on obedience and were temporary, finding their fulfillment in the Messiah, God's Son, who replaced the Old Mosaic Covenant with the New Covenant in His blood. Remember that God's ultimate purpose has always been salvation for sinners, and His choice of Israel was toward the accomplishment of that purpose. He called them to be an holy nation (see Exodus 19:5,6). Peter uses almost the same words of believers who were in the New Testament church, definitely including the Gentile believers, showing that it was not the physical seed of Abraham that was to be glorified, but the believers who would hear, believe and obey the Word of God (I Peter 2:9,10). When Paul says, "And so all Israel shall be saved" (Romans 11:26) he is not implying the glorification of the physical nation but rather the "turning away of ungodliness from Jacob" making them part of the believing, holy people who are saved by the blood of Christ.

3. In reading the Old Testament prophets, we must use common sense in applying them literally when they clearly apply to cities, nations and circumstances of the period in which the prophet was living. We need to remember, too, that the coming of the Messiah was the focal point of God's plan of salvation and of history and that much of Old Testament prophecy foretold the New Covenant spiritual blessings which God's people would enjoy through the finished work of Christ and the quickening, life-giving power of His Holy Spirit. Especially, we must accept the interpretation and application given to Old Testament prophecies by New Testament writers who were all guided by the Holy Spirit in what they wrote.

4. The Kingdom promises to David and his house were kept under God's providence in spite of tragic disobedience and sin for a thousand years of Israel's history and then were marvelously fulfilled in the Kingship of David's greater Son and in His everlasting, world-wide empire. From the day of Jesus' resurrection, He has been reigning, bringing His enemies under His feet and extending His Kingdom.

May I point out, for those who still cling to the hope of a millennial kingdom on this earth, that this prophecy concerning the "national" hope of salvation of the Jews before Jesus comes does not rob Christ of any of His glory. Rather, it enhances His Second Coming, recognizing it to be the climax of human history and the consummation of His present reign over this earth. At His coming, the dead will be raised and we shall all be changed, clothed with immortality. Death, the last enemy, will be swallowed up in victory and every authority and power will have been brought under His feet. This is when the final judgment will be held and the Kingdom will be delivered up to God the Father. Thank God, the promise is given that Israel still will have her day of grace and salvation and will gloriously complete the Church before Jesus comes. When He comes to take His own to Himself, it will be the end of the world and He will gather out of His Kingdom all who offend. At His coming, He promises to bring rest to believers who have endured troubles and vengeance to all who know not God and obey not the gospel (II Thessalonians 1:7,8).

5. The seventieth week of Daniel's prophecy in Daniel 9:24-27 was fulfilled in the time of Christ and has nothing to do with a future tribulation period or a covenant made by Anti-Christ, for the Messiah confirmed with many the covenant promised in Jeremiah 31:31-34. He brought to an end Israel's national witness under the Old Covenant, sending forth the gospel of salvation to all nations through the believing remnant of Jews who preached the Gospel of the Kingdom of Christ everywhere.

6. At the infinite cost of the suffering of His Own Son, God broke down the middle wall of partition between Jew and Gentile, making them one in Christ, bringing them both near to God, having made peace through the blood of His cross. Since He placed everyone, Jew and Gentile, under the

same covenant which alone can provide salvation, it is unreasonable and also contrary to the New Testament teaching to expect Him to revert to the Mosaic Covenant, which Scripture says could only fail, and use it for another period of history in dealing with sinners in this world.

7. God preserved the unique identity of the Jews through nineteen centuries of history, though they were scattered, often persecuted, and without a homeland. Now He has allowed them to return and build again a strong nation, even repossessing the city of Jerusalem in fulfillment of our Lord's definite prophecy. Therefore, we believe that He has something wonderful yet in store for them as a nation. He promises to remove the judgmental spiritual blindness which He has kept upon them for these centuries because of their continued rebellion and unwillingness to believe, and He promises to receive them in their fullness as life from the dead when they will at last believe on their Messiah. When the full number of Israelis have been grafted into their own olive tree, then He who is the only Life of that tree will come again to receive His completed and perfected Bride to Himself.

8. God did not set Israel aside during the church age to begin dealing with them again after the church is removed at the rapture. When the Mosaic Covenant proved its failure to give righteousness and salvation, God replaced it with the New Covenant in His Son Jesus, the Messiah. The fact that the nation rejected Jesus did not nullify the New Covenant nor did it leave Israel under the Old Mosaic Covenant. God placed the nation under the New Covenant and those who believed received life, salvation, son-ship; those who rejected His Son fell under judgment from which only faith in Christ can deliver. He has been dealing with the Jews ever since Calvary on the basis of the New Covenant and will continue to do so until Jesus comes. When He comes, it will be to give rest to His followers but also to take "vengeance on them that know not God and that obey not the gospel of our Lord Jesus Christ" (II Thessalonians 1:8). It will be too late at that time for one to hope to change his mind and believe on Jesus for salvation. This is why I believe He will deal with Israel in mercy before He comes for His Church.

Finally, we have seen the wonder of God's wisdom and the display of His infinite mercy in the interplay of Jew upon

Gentile and Gentile upon Jew in bringing His children into the kingdom of our Lord Jesus. God's plan of salvation for this world of sinners was able to turn the disobedience and sinful rebellion of the Jews against His Son to work for the salvation of Gentiles throughout the nations. And in the end time when the fullness of the Gentiles are come in, He will use them to provoke the Jews to jealousy so they will believe and come in. As the apostle says in Romans 11:30-32,

> For as ye in times past have not believed God, yet have now obtained mercy through their unbelief: Even so have these also now not believed, that through your mercy they also may obtain mercy. For God hath con-cluded them all in unbelief, that He might have mercy upon all.

He made peace through the blood of His cross, bringing Jew and Gentile into one body, fellow citizens with the saints and of the household of God. The Good Shepherd has found the lost sheep of the house of Israel and also the other sheep that were not of this fold (the Gentiles) and brought them in that there might be one fold and one Shepherd. And the completion of the Bride of Christ will be the crowning act of God's mercy when He removes the judgment from Israel and all who are called will be saved and brought into His Church.

PRAY FOR THE SALVATION OF ISRAEL

Again, may I lay upon your heart the burden to pray earnestly for God's mercy upon the Jews as we see the day of Christ's return approaching. Such a testimony before the world of the sudden conversion of multitudes in Israel would cause Christians to rejoice everywhere. At the same time, it could arouse the hatred ot those whose hearts are controlled by Satan and unleash a tempest of persecution which only God's power could enable His church to endure. He has promised that His own are sealed for all eternity, and we who belong to Him need not fear what man can do to us. Our God is able! The Lord Jesus is sovereign over heaven and earth and has the keys of death and of hell. His is the victory and the gates of hell cannot prevail against His Church. The Lord

Jesus is coming soon. Many signs indicate it but the primary one is the fulfilled prophecy of Israel back in the land controlling Jerusalem, and the time is ripe for God's mercy in saving grace to fall upon that nation. Pray that this may happen while it is still "the day of salvation." Pray that the Bride may be complete and ready when Jesus comes. Ask God to give you a heart that truly desires to see them saved and that will welcome them with Christ's love into the Body of Christ, His Church. God has given His Word, which cannot fail, that the judgment will be taken from Israel and in their "fullness" they will be received as "life from the dead." That day is coming and could come at any time. The return of Jesus has been delayed not because the Lord is slack concerning His promise; rather He "is longsuffering toward us, not willing that any should perish but that all should come to repentance" (II Peter 3:9).

In Isaiah 43 we find a beautiful passage spoken to Israel concerning God's grace in seeking out and restoring the seed of Israel from the Babylonian captivity. He did not bring all the physical seed back but qualifies which ones in these words, "even every one that is called by my name: for I have created him for my glory" (Isaiah 43:7). So, today, He who is completing the church, His Bride, will tarry until He has gathered from the seed of Israel "even every one that is called by My Name" and has restored them to His fold.

According to the prophecy of Jesus in Luke 21:24, the times of the Gentiles is fulfilled since Jerusalem is under the control of the Jews. We will know when "the fullness of the Gentiles" has come into the church only when we see a great work of repentance and faith in Jesus, their Messiah, accomplished by the Holy Spirit among the Jews. This will tell us that the judgment of spiritual blindness has at last been removed from Israel nationally. We will also know then that the Holy Spirit is preparing the Bride for the day of the coming of the Bridegroom and that He "is nigh, even at the doors."

JESUS IS COMING AGAIN

No one knows the day or the hour of the Second Coming of Jesus, our Saviour. We are told to watch and pray for we know not when the time is. But we are given signs and told that "when these things begin to come to pass, then look up and lift up your heads; for your redemption draweth nigh." Surely our present generation has enough indication in the swiftly occurring events in the Middle East to make us more earnest in keeping our own hearts prepared to meet our Lord and in sharing the gospel witness with those around us who have no faith and no hope of salvation through Christ. Let us pray that the nation that in the past 75 years bought its way and fought its way back into possession of the land will not find peace or satisfaction until they desire the "better land" that Abraham sought, the City of God, the heavenly Jerusalem wherein dwelleth righteousness through the precious blood of Jesus, their Messiah.

Then He will come again. Even so come, Lord Jesus.

APPENDIX A
Prophecy and Fulfillment

There is no doubt in the mind of anyone who believes the Bible to be the Word of God that God is true and cannot lie; that what He has promised to do He will surely fulfill; that when He foretells an event, it is bound to happen. But there is a great deal of confusion among Christian teachers of the Scriptures when it becomes a matter of interpreting prophecies and promises, especially in the Old Testament, and even in some passages of the New Testament.

The confusion arises from the difficulty of interpreting the exact meaning of a prophecy and the application of the words to their material or spiritual fulfillment. These difficulties can be classified under the following headings and we shall try to use illustration to point up the problems and the method of solution:

A. Different meanings in the usage of certain words or phrases.

B. Passages in the New Testament that specifically declare the fulfillment of an Old Testament prophecy but are not accepted as truly or fully fulfilled.

C. Passages where an interpreter establishes his opinion as the only possible interpretation of a prophecy or promise and requires that the fulfillment be exactly as he thinks, or else it is not a true fulfillment.

D. Passages where there is both literal and spiritual fulfillment of the prophecy.

Let us look then at some of these problems and especially try to see how the Word of God expresses fulfillment.

A. Different meanings in the usage of certain words or phrases.

1. Consider the word "everlasting" as it is used in the covenant and promise given to Abraham. He was told that all

the land of Canaan would be given unto him and to his seed for an everlasting possession (Genesis 17:8). Immediately after this, God gave Abraham the covenant of circumcision (Genesis 17:9-14) and said, "and My covenant shall be in your flesh for an everlasting covenant" (v. 13). Now obviously a covenant having to do with a piece of material property on a physical earth, especially when the earth is reserved for judgment by fire, with the promise of a new heaven and a new earth, cannot be meant to be "everlasting" in the complete sense of the word. Nor is the covenant of circumcision to be taken as an "everlasting" covenant in the fullest sense of the word because the New Testament teaches that circumcision of the flesh is of no avail but is superceded by the spiritual circumcision of the heart (Romans 2:28-29). Furthermore, the Sabbath was instituted as an "everlasting" sign that Israel was God's chosen nation, and yet this was superceded by the Lord's Day which is observed not by commandment but out of love and appreciation of the Risen Lord. Other feasts of Israel were commanded to be kept as an "everlasting" observance, such as Passover and Pentecost which were done away when the Mosaic Covenant was abrogated and replaced through Jesus, the Mediator of a better covenant.

Surely this is sufficient to make us more careful in determining the usage of a word that may have different meanings. The word "everlasting" obviously is used with the meaning of "perpetual" (so long as a covenant was to be in force) and not always in the sense of eternal. We shall deal more with this subject as we consider the important covenant and promise given by God to Abraham.

2. Another term in prophetic writing that illustrates a different cause of confusion in the interpretation of its fulfillment is found in Malachi 4:5,6 concerning the sending of Elijah "before the coming of the great and dreadful day of the Lord." Some take this to mean a literal return of the ancient prophet Elijah just before the end of the world. Others find the prophecy fulfilled by John the Baptist who prepared the way before the coming of Jesus, the Messiah. Now, unless one insists on one single meaning for the phrase "the great and dreadful Day of the Lord," it is not difficult to accept the plain words of Jesus declaring the prophecy to be fulfilled by the coming of John the Baptist (Matthew 11:14; 17:10-13). Yet

there are some to whom the "Day of the Lord" can only refer to the Second Coming of Christ and, therefore, who still are looking for a fulfillment of the prophecy with an actual return of Elijah in person. One has only to take a concordance and look up in the Old Testament the references where this phrase is used to see that the "Day of the Lord" refers to His coming in judgment whether upon Israel, upon Judah, upon Babylon or upon Egypt and so can very well mean the day of vengeance and visitation upon Jerusalem in 70 A.D. In Matthew 17:11, Our Lord confirms that the scribes were right in saying that "Elijah is come already" and verse 13 says that the disciples understood that He spake of John the Baptist. How could Jesus be more explicit?

3. A very important and intensely interesting study is the usage of words and phrases under the Old and the New Covenants to express the blessings of God for His people. Again, may I urge you to keep in mind that the Old Mosaic Covenant was fulfilled by our Lord Jesus and in its place, for Israel, the New Covenant was confirmed by the sacrifice and resurrection of Israel's Messiah, the Lord Jesus Christ. Many of the prophets, in describing the return from the Assyrian and Babylonian captivity, use terms of material blessing, security, abundance, and perpetuity for the nation when they were led back by their covenant God to the land and to the city of Jerusalem. But they not only spoke of the blessings of the restored nation under the Old Covenant; their words are full of promise of the greater blessings under the New Covenant, which blessings could not be described adequately except in terms that foreshadowed and typified greater things to come.

For Israel to be back in the land applied to the days of the Old Covenant, for it was their home and the place of worship. When Christ confirmed the New Covenant, citizenship was no longer in the "land" but in heaven, and worship was in the heavenly Jerusalem, the city of the Living God.

Israel was promised that they would never be plucked off the land again and God kept His promise until it was fulfilled in Christ who said, "I give unto them eternal life; and they shall never perish, neither shall any man pluck them out of my hand" (John 10:28). The words of the Old Covenant which promised to the returning captives that they would "hunger no more neither thirst any more," were fulfilled supremely under the New Covenant in the words of Jesus, "I am the bread of life: he that cometh to me shall never hunger; and he that believeth on me shall never thirst" (John 6:35).

The promise of prosperity spoken in terms such as "eat ye that which is good and let your soul delight itself in fatness" or "the reaper shall overtake the ploughman" is fulfilled in something infinitely better under the New Covenant in the words of our Lord, "I am come that they might have life and that they might have it more abundantly" (John 10:10b).

A phrase like, "they shall beat their swords into plough-shares" can be compared with the New Covenant words, "a new commandment I give unto you, that ye love one another"; or "the lion and the lamb shall lie down together" with "there is neither Jew nor Greek, there is neither bond nor free, there is neither male nor female: for ye are all one in Christ Jesus"; or Isaiah's words, "and an highway shall be there, and a way, and it shall be called the way of holiness" (Isaiah 35:8) compared with Hebrews 10:19,20, "having, therefore, brethren, boldness to enter into the holiest by the blood of Jesus, by a new and living way" or John 14:6, "Jesus said unto him, I am the way, the truth, the life; no man cometh unto the Father but by Me"; or finally, the peace and security promised to the returned captives fulfilled in the words of the Saviour, "Peace I leave with you, My peace I give unto you…" (John 14:27). Remember that Jesus fulfilled the hope and promise of the Old Covenant in Himself and at the same time confirmed with Israel (all who would believe) the New Covenant bringing to them righteousness, salvation, and everlasting life.

B. Passages in the New Testament that specifically declare fulfillment of an Old Testament prophecy but are not accepted as truly fulfilled.

This illustration concerns the prophecy, "They shall look upon Me whom they have pierced." The prophet Zechariah had said,

> And I will pour upon the house of David and upon the inhabitants of Jerusalem the spirit of grace and of supplications: and they shall look upon me whom they have pierced and they shall mourn for him as one

mourneth for his only son and shall be in bitterness for him, as one that is in bitterness for his firstborn (Zechariah 12:10-12).

Many Bible teachers look for this prophecy to be fulfilled at some yet future date when Israel will look upon Jesus when He returns and they will believe as a nation. It is strange that they can ignore the definite statement of the Apostle John as he records the crucifixion of Jesus in his gospel (John 19:36,37): "For these things were done that the scripture should be fulfilled, a bone of Him shall not be broken. And again another scripture saith, They shall look on Him whom they pierced." John says this scripture was fulfilled when Jesus hung on the cross.

Think of the anguish and bitterness of the Jews who were pricked in their heart on the Day of Pentecost and realized what they had done to God's Son. Zechariah rightly describes their grief, not as a national mourning, for the nation would reject Him, but with individual families expressing their grief separately (Zechariah 12:12-14). Furthermore, in the next chapter, verse 1 of Zechariah 13, the prophet says, "In that day there shall be a fountain opened to the House of David and to the inhabitants of Jerusalem for sin and for uncleanness," which certainly was fulfilled when Jesus died on Calvary's cross, identifying "in that day" as the day of Christ's first coming.

However, there is still another future prophecy in Revelation 1:7, which declares, "Behold he cometh with clouds: and every eye shall see Him, and they also which pierced Him: and all kindreds of the earth shall wail because of Him." This is yet to be fulfilled, but it is quite different from Zechariah's prophecy which John so clearly states was fulfilled when the Jews saw "Him whom they pierced" on the cross. Certainly, we ought to accept the New Testament teaching of how and when an Old Testament prophecy was fulfilled. Zechariah's prophecy was fulfilled at the cross and there is no warrant to say it is yet to be fulfilled.

I stress this point because I believe it is fundamental to a correct understanding of the interpretation of prophecy. When we accept the teaching of the New Testament writers, who were taught by our Lord and inspired by the Holy Spirit, as to when and how Old Testament prophecies are fulfilled, we will have a basis for a proper understanding of the relation of the church to the plan of salvation revealed through Old Testament prophets and through Israel's history. On the other hand, if we refuse their clear teaching and try to fit it into our preconceived ideas, we can be led far astray. The above is a good illustration, for by refusing John's plain statement regarding the fulfillment of Zechariah's prophecy, many have been led to a false hope of Israel's national conversion by looking on Jesus with physical eyes at His Second Coming. This is totally without Scriptural authority.

C. Passages where an interpreter establishes his own opinion as the only possible interpretation of a prophecy or promise and requires that the fulfillment be exactly as he thinks, or it is not a true fulfillment.

1. One of the most important Old Testament prophecies that has been seriously misinterpreted is Amos 9:11, quoted by James, the leader of the Jerusalem church, in Acts 15:15-17. In Acts 15 we have the report of the leaders of the early church gathered in the Jerusalem conference to investigate the question of the inclusion of the Gentiles in the church of our Lord Jesus. Were Gentiles to be required to submit to the legalistic rites of Judaism and come under the yoke of the law or could Gentiles be welcomed into the household of faith simply by believing in and accepting Jesus as Lord and Saviour?

The Apostle Peter testified to his experience of preaching in a Gentile house and seeing the Holy Spirit witness to their acceptance into the fellowship of believers. Paul and Barnabas told of their joy at seeing the Holy Spirit giving the gifts of grace and salvation to Gentiles without requiring any rite or legal ceremony. Then James, the leader of the church in Jerusalem acknowledged the facts presented by Peter and Paul and said that they were in perfect harmony with the voice of prophecy. He then quotes the prophecy of Amos 9:11 saying:

> And to this agree the words of the prophets: as it is written, 'After this I will return and will build again the tabernacle of David, which is fallen down; and I will build again the ruins thereof and I will set it up: That the residue of men might seek after the Lord and all the

Gentiles upon whom my name is called, saith the Lord, who doeth all these things.'

This quotation from Amos is intended to bring into agreement with Old Testament prophecy the inclusion of Gentiles among those who are called by the Name of the Lord and, therefore, authorizes by the Scriptures the acceptance of the Gentiles.

The interpretation of this passage hinges on the meaning of the words "after this." In fact, Amos did not use the phrase "after this," but said, "In that day" which by the Old Testament prophets often means "in the day of the Messiah." Amos was simply stating that in a future day called "that day" the Lord would come again and build up the tabernacle of David which was fallen. Then as James quotes the prophecy, "The residue of men might seek after the Lord and all the Gentiles upon whom my name is called." There is absolutely no indication that the words "after this" or "in that day" have nothing to do with Gentile salvation. That comes after David's Tabernacle or House is built up and then the great inclusion of Gentiles would be accomplished. Since there is no question but what the Gentiles have been included in the household of faith since shortly after Pentecost, we must conclude that David's Tabernacle was already rebuilt by Jesus when James spoke at the Jerusalem conference.

Still there are many Bible teachers who relate the prophecy of Amos to a later period, *after this*, meaning after the church age, simply because they do not believe that Jesus literally "built again the Tabernacle of David."

The question we must decide then is whether or not we can believe that Jesus, during His life and ministry, rebuilt the House of David. Of course, if one assumes or postulates the meaning of "rebuilding the House of David" to include restoring a visible earthly Kingdom to the House of David and sitting upon David's actual throne in the city of Jerusalem, ruling the nations of the world for a thousand years, then the prophecy was not fulfilled by Jesus of Nazareth and we must regard it all as yet to occur in the future.

However, take a serious look at what Jesus did for the House and Kingdom of David when He came long ago: (a) The Scriptures definitely trace His ancestry according to the flesh back to King David. For most of the past 600 years before His birth, the House of David was fallen and had lain in ruins. Jesus brought more glory to Israel and the House of David than all the 26 sons of David who had sat upon the throne in Jerusalem during nearly 500 years of history before the Babylonian Captivity. (b) Jesus entered into the city of Jerusalem with a triumphal procession of followers acclaiming Him to be the Son of David. (c) Before Pilate, He confessed that He was a King but said, "My Kingdom is not of this world." (d) He hung upon a cross of shame but the title above His head declared Him to be Jesus of Nazareth, the King of the Jews, and Pilate would not alter what he had written. (e) After His resurrection, He gathered more than 500 followers to a mountain top in Galilee and claimed that all authority in heaven and earth had been given to Him. (f) The apostles and the early church went everywhere preaching the Kingdom of God and every believer has been translated into the Kingdom of our Lord Jesus Christ. (g) St. Paul said over 1900 years ago that "Christ must reign until He has put all enemies under His feet" (I Corinthians 15:25). For over 1900 years from His throne in glory, Christ has administered His Kingdom and controlled the nations and empires of the world. If all authority was given to our Lord at His resurrection, then who else but the Lord Jesus Christ has "put down the mighty from their seats and exalted them of low degree"? (h) Isaiah 9:6 had foretold of the Son that was to be given that "the government should be upon His shoulder" and

of the increase of His government and peace there shall be no end, upon the throne of David, and upon His kingdom, to order it, and to establish it with judgment and with justice from henceforth even forever.

The fulfillment of the prophecy that He would build again the House of David is not nullified because He didn't occupy a physical throne in Jerusalem requiring Herod to abdicate so He could sit there. The prophecy was fulfilled in the supreme honor brought to the House of David when God's Son became flesh and when on the cross He sealed a covenant that established His right to rule the world and call forth His inheritance from all the nations on earth into His everlasting Kingdom. This is far greater than anything David could have hoped for as he thought of the promise of God to his house.

Jesus established His Kingdom by rebuilding the house of David and restoring its fortunes for His reign over the believing remnant of the house of Jacob. His Father who set Him upon His Holy Hill of Zion had also said, "Ask of Me and I will give thee the heathen for thine inheritance and the uttermost parts of the earth for Thy possession" (Psalm 2:8). So He reached out His arms of love to gather into His Kingdom the outcasts, the bruised, the afflicted, the struggling of all nations of every class and kindred who would respond to Him in love. For this reason, James at the Jerusalem conference, quoted the words of Amos to show their agreement and fulfillment in the gathering of Gentiles into the Church of Jesus Christ, together with believing Jews, simply on the basis of true faith.

2. Another very significant Old Testament prophecy which the New Testament interprets is Joel 2:28-32. This passage quoted by Peter in Acts 2:16-21 is said to be fulfilled in the pouring out of the Holy Spirit on the Day of Pentecost. The disciples had left the upper room filled with the Spirit and declared the joyous news of Jesus' resurrection in tongues that could be understood by people of many nations who were gathered in Jerusalem for the Feast of Pentecost. Some said that the disciples were drunk, but Peter stood forth and explained they were not drunk but were filled with the Holy Spirit of God which He had shed forth even as He promised through the prophet Joel.

Peter quotes the prophet's words spoken some 800 years before, saying

> This is that which was spoken by the prophet Joel: And it shall come to pass in the last days saith God, I will pour out of my Spirit upon all flesh: and your sons and your daughters shall prophesy and your young men shall see visions and your old men shall dream dreams: and on my servants and on my handmaidens I will pour out in those days of my spirit and they shall prophesy: And I will show wonders in the heaven above, and signs in the earth beneath: blood and fire and vapour of smoke: the sun shall be turned into darkness and the moon into blood before that great and notable day of the Lord come. And it shall come to pass that whosoever shall call upon the name of the Lord shall be saved (Acts 2:16-21 and Joel 2:28-32).

This is an important illustration of the way the New Testament interprets the fulfillment of Old Testament prophecy and we are wise to follow the guidance of the Holy Spirit. James teaches us that the term "the last days" as used in the Old Testament does not necessarily refer to the final days of this world's history, but may also apply to the entire period of history which began with the New Covenant in Christ. Certainly the pouring out of the Spirit upon all flesh was fulfilled and the opening of the door of salvation to all who will call on the name of the Lord was likewise fulfilled and is still being accomplished. Since the beginning and the end of Joel's prophecy was fulfilled in the apostle's day, we can be reasonably certain that the great and notable Day of the Lord foretold by the prophet was the day of God's judgment upon Israel in 70 A.D. when His wrath was visited upon them to the uttermost (I Thessalonians 2:16). If we demand literal fulfillment of the signs and portents in heaven and earth, surely the Star of Bethlehem and the darkened sun over Calvary ought to satisfy us that God is true to His Word. I can see no reason for Dr. Scofield in his edition of the Holy Bible to break the prophet's words after verse 29 of Joel chapter 2 and insert "5. The signs preceding the second advent and the day of the Lord" when the prophecy clearly declares the deliverance of all who shall call on the name of the Lord, certainly referring to this age of the church and not a post-rapture period. At least we know that the Spirit was shed forth "in these last days" and the open door of salvation was in fulfillment of God's Word spoken through the prophet Joel 800 years before it came to pass. How wonderful!

3. A New Testament passage, Acts 4:24-28, declares the fulfillment of Psalm 2, but there are many who teach that this Psalm is yet to be fulfilled. The disciples had been threatened by the Sanhedrin with severe punishment if they continued preaching the resurrection of Jesus. They were let go, and returning to the disciples they lifted up their voice with one accord and said,

Lord, thou art God which hast made heaven and earth and the sea and all that in them is; who by the mouth of Thy servant David hast said, 'Why do the heathen rage and the people imagine vain things? The Kings of the earth stood up and the rulers were gathered together

164

against the Lord and against His Christ.' For of a truth against thy Holy child Jesus, whom thou hast anointed, both Herod and Pontius Pilate with the Gentiles and the people of Israel were gathered together, for to do whatsoever Thy hand and Thy counsel determined before to be done.

Here we have a clear statement in the New Testament uttered in a prayer that caused the place to be shaken and brought a mighty infilling of the Holy Spirit which tells us that the prophecy of David in Psalm 2 has been fulfilled. Yet there are many who object and say that the fulfillment was not literal and therefore there must come a future day when Jesus will find the nations arrayed against Him and God will set Him upon the Davidic throne in the millennial kingdom. When Scripture says that a prophecy is fulfilled, I believe we ought to accept it. It seems to me that it is only blind prejudice that makes one fail to see the wonderful way in which Psalm 2 was fulfilled by God in the day when Jesus came to His own.

Look at the fulfillment: (a) The enemies of Christ tried to do their worst, even putting Him to death upon the cross, but God held them in derision. Everything they did to His Son was in fulfillment of prophecy. (b) God did declare Jesus to be His Son; (c) God did place Him upon His holy Hill of Zion as the King of Kings and the law of Christ's Kingdom has ever since gone forth from Jerusalem; (d) God did grant Him the heathen for His inheritance and the title deed to the world itself is His; and (e) Jesus has been "ruling the nations with a rod of iron and dashing them in pieces like a potter's vessel" (witness Rome in the fourth century, Hitler's Germany, Mussolini's Italy, etc.). Who has been sovereign over this world since Calvary if it hasn't been the Lord Jesus Christ, who was given all authority "in heaven and in earth" (Matthew 28:19)? Or was St. Paul wrong when he said that "He must reign until He hath put all enemies under His feet"? (I Corinthians 15:25). It is dangerous for anyone to demand that prophecy must be fulfilled in a certain way before it can be regarded as fulfilled and who, therefore, refuses to accept the fulfillment which is plainly recorded even in Scripture.

D. Passages where there is both literal and spiritual fulfillment of the prophecy.

I shall include one more illustration of the kind of confusion which results when a completely literal interpretation of a prophecy is demanded that obviously is intended to be both literally and spiritually fulfilled. Zechariah, writing over 500 years before Jesus came prophesied, saying,

> Then shall the Lord go forth and fight against those nations as when He fought in the day of battle. And His feet shall stand in that day upon the Mount of Olives which is before Jerusalem on the east and the Mount of Olives shall cleave in the midst thereof toward the east and toward the west and there shall be a very great valley (Zechariah 14:3,4).

Now Jesus did stand upon the Mount of Olives when He was here on earth and there was a great earthquake when He died on Calvary, but the Mount of Olives was not literally split in half causing a deep valley running east and west. How then shall we understand the fulfillment of this prophecy? Must we put this all into the future since we cannot find a literal fulfillment of the cleavage of the mountain and the fleeing of the people to Azal to escape the disaster of the quake?

I find it impossible to believe that a literal meeting is required of the people fleeing for safety through the cloven Mount of Olives. When the Lord of heaven and earth returns in His glory, who is the Shield and Protector of His people, what possible reason can there be for His people to have to flee like refugees through a valley to Azal (a place probably not far from Jerusalem but without any definite identification today)? Why would they flee? And from whom would they flee if Jesus is in the city of Jerusalem?

Those who teach this seem to ignore the type of language used in prophecy to express spiritual realities in material or physical terms. (a) Consider the familiar words of Isaiah 40:3,4 which, without doubt, refer to the time of John the Baptist who prepared for the coming of Jesus:

> The voice of him that crieth in the wilderness. Prepare ye the way of the Lord, make straight in the desert a highway for our God. Every valley shall be exalted and

every mountain and hill shall be made low; and the crooked shall be made straight and the rough places plain.

These words were not fulfilled literally but with some perception of spiritual reality we can understand the preparation that was made for the coming of God's Son and His brief pilgrimage on earth. (b) Or consider the great hope set before Israel in these glowing words by Isaiah:

For since the beginning of the world men have not heard nor perceived by the ear, neither have seen, O God, beside Thee, what He hath prepared for him that waiteth for Him (Isaiah 64:4).

Are these promises of material blessings prepared for the nation of Israel? Not at all. In I Corinthians 2:9, the apostle quotes these words of Isaiah and then adds, "But God hath revealed them unto us by His Spirit: for the Spirit searcheth all things, yea the deep things of God." Obviously Paul is referring to the spiritual blessings in Christ revealed to all believers who truly love God.

Therefore, we must be very careful to interpret Scripture as God's Word reveals His truth and must recognize that God through the prophets was primarily concerned to reveal the plan of redemption wrought by His Son.

Returning, then, to the prophecy of Zechariah, it is important that in understanding the fulfillment of these words, "His feet shall stand in that day upon the Mount of Olives" we look at the context in which they are placed. Therefore, we quote here the entire passage of Zechariah 13:7-14:9:

Awake, O sword against my shepherd and against the man that is my fellow, saith the Lord of Hosts: smite the shepherd, and the sheep shall be scattered: and I will turn mine hand upon the little ones. And it shall come to pass, that in all the land, saith the Lord, two parts theein shall be cut off and die; but the third shall be left therein shall be cut off and die; but the third shall be left and will refine them as silver is refined, and will try them as gold is tried: they shall call on my name and I will hear them: I will say, It is my people: and they shall say, The Lord is my God. Behold the day of the Lord cometh and thy spoil shall be divided in the midst of thee. For I will gather all nations against Jerusalem to battle: and the city shall be taken, and the houses rifled, and the women ravished; and half of the city shall go forth into captivity and the residue of the people shall not be cut off from the city. Then shall the Lord go forth and fight against those nations as when He fought in the day of battle.

And His feet shall stand in that day upon the Mount of Olives, which is before Jerusalem on the east and the Mount of Olives shall cleave in the midst thereof toward the east and toward the west, and there shall be a very great valley; and half of the mountain shall remove toward the north, and half of it toward the south. And ye shall flee to the valley of the mountains; for the valley of the mountains shall reach unto Azal [the Hebrew word means "noble"]: yea, ye shall flee, like as ye fled from before the earthquake in the days of Uzziah King of Judah: and the Lord my God shall come, and all the saints with thee. And it shall come to pass in that day that the light shall not be clear, nor dark: But it shall be one day which shall be known to the Lord, not day, nor night: but it shall come to pass that at evening time it shall be light. And it shall be in that day, that living waters shall go out from Jerusalem; half of them toward the former sea and half of them toward the hinder sea: in summer and in winter shall it be. And the Lord shall be king over all the earth: in that day shall there be one Lord, and His name one.

Going back to verse 7 of chapter 13 (of course the prophet made no chapter divisions), we find a prophecy which was quoted by our Lord and said to be fulfilled in His day:

Awake, O sword against my shepherd and against the man that is my fellow, saith the Lord of Hosts: smite the shepherd and the sheep shall be scattered and I will turn mine hand upon my little ones.

Were these words literally fulfilled? Did God use His sword against the shepherd? Did He literally turn His hand upon His little ones? When we look at Matthew 26:30,31 (also Mark 14:26,27), it is most interesting to note that Jesus was standing on the Mount of Olives when He quoted Zechariah's words for there we read,

> And when they had sung an hymn they went out into the Mount of Olives. Then saith Jesus unto them, 'All ye shall be offended because of me this night: for it is written, I will smite the shepherd and the sheep of the flock shall be scattered abroad.'

Following on in Zechariah 13, verses 8 and 9, the destruction is foretold that would come on two-thirds of the population of the land with one-third "who call on My Name" being brought "through the fire" and kept as God's people. Surely this was literally fulfilled in the period closing with 70 A.D., the destruction of Jerusalem by Titus. Then in verses 1 and 2 of chapter 14, Zechariah is more specific in his prophecy, calling that day "the Day of the Lord" and declaring that it is God's judgment in bringing the nations against Jerusalem and the destruction is complete. How tragic if we are required to take this as an unfulfilled prophecy and that we must still anticipate a day when God again

> gathers all nations against Jerusalem to battle; and the city shall be taken and the houses rifled and the women ravished and half of the city shall go forth into captivity.

But this was fulfilled so completely in 70 A.D. by Rome, the mistress of the world, with all nations represented in Titus' army that, thank God, we don't need to look for another destruction of Jerusalem yet to come.

Continuing, Zechariah 14:3 says, "Then shall the Lord go forth and fight against those nations, as when He fought in the day of battle." Does this mean that after Jerusalem was laid waste, the Lord went out to fight literal battles against the nations that destroyed the city, or is the prophet referring to a different kind of conquest? In verse 7 chapter 13, Jesus is foretold as the smitten shepherd. But at the same time that He was "smitten of God" He was waging a battle on the cross against the powers of darkness and against Satan himself. After His resurrection, He went forth with the sword of His mouth (God's Word) to conquer the nations and bring His subjects from every tribe and nation into His everlasting Kingdom.

The Saviour literally fulfilled the prophetic words in Zechariah 14:4 that "his feet shall stand in that day upon the Mount of Olives" but the rest of the prophecy is better understood as foretelling His mighty work of redemption. He did provide a way, "a new and living way," by which men can flee to the safety and security of eternal salvation (verses 4 and 5).

Next, in verses 6 and 7, the description of a particular day seems to refer to the day of the crucifixion when at noontime the darkness of night fell for three hours and then with the cry, "It is finished," light came at evening time. The day when God gave His Son to die for sinners was the strangest day of history, "one day which shall be known to the Lord, not day, nor night." Verse 8 follows next and reads,

> And it shall come to pass in that day that living waters shall go out from Jerusalem half of them toward the former sea and half of them toward the hinder sea: in summer and in winter it shall be.

From the cross has flowed the stream of living water that has quenched the thirst of all who have come to drink of this precious fountain of the water of life. It seems to me quite impossible to imagine that this could prophesy an actual literal flowing stream of material water when the prophet declares it to be "living" water. The New Testament makes it abundantly clear that in Jesus' death and resurrection He provides spiritual water and when a man drinks of this, he shall never thirst again, but as Jesus says, "the water that I shall give him shall be in him a well of water springing up unto everlasting life" (John 14:4).

And finally, Zechariah 14:9 says, "And the Lord shall be king over all the earth; in that day shall there be one Lord and His Name one." This too was fulfilled when Jesus rose victorious from the grave, for He was given all authority in heaven and earth and began His reign and the subjugation of all nations. I wonder if St. Paul had this verse of Zechariah in mind when he says in Ephesians 4:4,5, "There is one body and one spirit even as ye are called in one hope of your calling; one Lord, one faith, one baptism."

I believe that this prophecy, when studied carefully, illustrates the two-fold fulfillment of Old Testament prophecies, partly in literal actual historical events and partly in spiritual realities of which the economy of the Old Covenant was a shadow. From the Scriptures the apostles were able to convince many in Israel that Jesus was the very Messiah, the Hope of Israel and of the world, and the fulfillment of prophecy was the most convincing proof of this great truth.

How wonderful was the careful preparation for the coming of the Redeemer through the Mosaic Covenant and the Holy Scriptures. And yet how tragic that His own people rejected Him and missed the day of His visitation because they refused to believe the Scriptures and looked for an earthly Kingdom rather than for the Saviour from sin and the Lord of Glory. We should be warned today and not be guilty of trying to make the Scriptures a pre-written newspaper of today's world and national events instead of a book revealing God's plan of salvation.

Comments on Revelation 20:1-9 Regarding the Millennium

1. With respect to Satan being bound, three things must be said:

A. There is no indication that the angel has to struggle with or defeat Satan when he binds him with the chain and casts him into the abyss. Evidently, he was already defeated, the victory having been won by the Saviour when He died on the cross. As far as deceiving and controlling the nations, he was bound, for the nations were now given into the hands of Jesus, the King of Kings (Psalm 2).

B. In Revelation 20:1-3, we read that he was bound and thrown into the abyss "so that he should not deceive the nations any longer" but after the millennium he would be released for a short time. Verses 7-9 continue saying that when he is released he will come out to deceive the nations and gather them for a final assault upon the people of God and the beloved city. Note that he has been bound with respect to "deceiving the nations" and when let loose will be able to deceive them for the final conflict. He evidently is allowed some liberty to tempt and to work evil in the hearts of men because during the church age Christians have been subject to a warfare against spiritual wickedness and power (see Ephesians 6:10-12).

C. Speaking of Satan's kingdom, our Lord says, "No one can enter a strong man's house and plunder his property unless he first binds the strong man." He clearly teaches that in order to deliver Satan's children from his kingdom He had to bind Satan and then He could set them free and bring them into His own Kingdom of light and truth (Mark 3:23-27). He has kept Satan bound for 19 centuries while He has been translating His subjects into the Kingdom of God's Beloved Son (Colossians 1:13).

2. In Revelation 20:4, those who lived and reigned with Him are the souls of those who were beheaded for their witness

and who had refused to worship the beast and the image and did not have the mark of the beast. (The mark of the beast may be in contrast to the marks of the Lord Jesus which the apostle Paul said he bore in his own body (Galatians 6:17). Regardless, it evidently means those who were faithful to the Lord and died and were waiting the "redemption of the body" at the rapture. This definitely puts the millennium before the rapture.

3. Revelation 20:5: The first resurrection takes place not at the rapture but at the time of the conversion of a sinner from the death of sin to the life of righteousness. In John's Gospel, chapter 5:24-29, he quotes Jesus who clearly teaches two resurrections. The first, a resurrection to life when one hears and believes His Word; the second, a resurrection of the body from the grave. This second resurrection is "the redemption of the body" which takes place at the coming of Christ or at the rapture. The second resurrection includes all who have died, both good and bad. That is why John says those who have part in the first resurrection are blessed because the second death, the death of the soul, has no power over them. Again, this puts the period of their reign with Christ before His triumphant Second Coming.

4. What reason is there for Jesus to reign on this earth over people and nations who are still living with unredeemed fleshly natures? Do we expect Him to prove that by His physical presence He can do something He failed to do by His Holy Spirit? The natural man cannot know the things of God for they are spiritually discerned (I Corinthians 2:14). God's Word teaches that to be a part of Christ's Kingdom the natural man must die to self, be crucified with Christ, be born again, be raised from the death of sin to the life of righteousness. God's Word is very plain that He will never force a person to be righteous against his will by the law. The law cannot give life even if it is administered by Jesus in person. Read Revelation and see how even the awful judgments and plagues described in John's visions do not bring men to repentance but only make them curse God the more. The picture of Jesus with "a rod of iron" in His hand "dashing" the unbelieving and unrighteous nations "in pieces like a potter's vessel" does not belong to His final Kingdom but fits perfectly with His present reign over the world since His resurrection while He has sent His ambassa-

174

dors into all nations to call believers everywhere into His everlasting Kingdom. He has been reigning for nearly two thousand years now breaking down empires, raising up new nations, overturning the unrighteous and preserving His own in the midst of trials and persecutions.

5. The millennial kingdom is supposed to be on this earth with people of flesh and blood existing in their natural state, many of whom are not redeemed. However, God's Word in I Corinthians 15:50 says plainly that flesh and blood cannot inherit the Kingdom of God nor can the perishable inherit the imperishable. Moreover, if Jesus reigns in perfect righteousness over the nations for a thousand years, how can Satan find so many ("the number of whom is as the sand of the sea") who will gather against the camp of the saints and the beloved city for war? During the millennium they are supposed to study war no more, yet Satan finds an innumerable army ready to fight!

6. The Coming of our Lord Jesus with the great events which take place in connection with His coming leaves no place or time for a thousand-year reign on this earth following His coming.

a. At His coming, death will be swallowed up in victory (I Corinthians 15:51-54). All that are in the grave will hear His voice and come forth, some to everlasting life and some to everlasting destruction (John 5:28,29). How can there be a further exercise of death's power if the resurrection day means his destruction? Death is the final enemy to be brought under the feet of Christ. It is hard to conceive the mighty power that will be manifest in finally breaking the bands of death and freeing all who have been held under its sway.

b. At His coming, there will be separation of the believer from the unbeliever or the good from the bad. II Thessalonians 1:6-10 teaches that when He comes He will give rest to His own but vengeance on all who know not God and who obey not the gospel. Jesus teaches (Matthew 13:37-43) that the tares and wheat would grow together until the end of the world (or age) when they would be separated. The tares, representing the evil ones in His Kingdom (the world) would be gathered for destruction but the wheat (the righteous) would shine forth as the sun in the Kingdom of their Father.

Who then, if the good are taken and the bad are destroyed, will be left to be subjects on earth in the millennial kingdom?

c. In connection with His coming, creation will be freed from the curse of sin. This is taught in Romans 8:18-23 where Paul says that creation waits eagerly for the revealing of the sons of God, groaning while we wait for our adoption as sons, the redemption of the body. And, clearly, the "redemption of our body" will take place at His coming for us. Remember that our Lord cannot come for His saints without bringing with Him His saints; they are at present with Christ but without bodies and according to I Thessalonians 4:14,16 they must be raised first to participate in the rapture.

d. At Jesus' coming, the heavens will pass away with a roar, the elements will be destroyed with intense heat and the earth and its works will be burned up. We look for new heavens and a new earth wherein dwelleth righteousness (II Peter 3:10).

7. How is it that if the millennial kingdom on earth is such a glorious prospect for Israel and for the world, Paul fails to mention it when outlining the consummation of Christ's work in I Corinthians 15:20-28? The resurrection of Christ is declared, then the resurrection of Christ's at His coming and next comes the end, when He delivers up the Kingdom to God the Father. This deliverance of the Kingdom to God occurs when Christ has abolished all rule and authority and power and put all His enemies under His feet. Psalm 110:1 says that Christ would sit at God's right hand until He put all enemies under His feet. This plainly declares that He was ruling from the heavenly throne not on earth in the millennial kingdom, while this subduing of His enemies was taking place. Note that the last enemy destroyed and brought under His feet is death and that Paul clearly puts the destruction of death at the time of the rapture (resurrection). This means that all Christ's enemies are brought under His feet when He destroys death, i.e., when He comes to redeem the body from the power of death by the resurrection. There is no mention of the millennial kingdom but only that Christ will deliver the kingdom that He has won to the Father that God may be all in all.

8. Why then does John in his vision speak of a thousand-

year reign? We must remember that when John was given his vision, no one but the Father in heaven knew how long Jesus would reign from the time of His resurrection until the day of His second coming, the day of our resurrection. The souls of martyred and faithful believers have lived and reigned with Christ over the earth during this period which has continued for 19 centuries. The end has been delayed because God is longsuffering, not willing that any should perish (II Peter 3:9). Thus, John, seeing in vision the scope of this entire period completing the plan of redemption and establishing the worldwide Kingdom of Christ, uses the term thousand years to express long duration and yet the certain, final completion of the period of Christ's reign over this world. Remember that Peter says that "with the Lord one day is as a thousand years and a thousand years as one day" (II Peter 3:8).

Different Views On Certain Prophetic Events

My grandfather, William E. Blackstone, was truly a servant of God and was privileged to further missionary work and evangelism throughout the world during the last half of his long life. His book, *Jesus is Coming*, written in 1878, has sold well over a million copies and still is awakening the interest of many readers to study the prophetic teachings in the Word of God concerning the Second Coming of our Lord Jesus Christ. I share heartily in his emphasis on the Blessed Hope of Christ's coming but since there are some things about which we disagree, the following comparison will make more clear the differences that exist between us.

JESUS IS COMING W.E. Blackstone	ISRAEL'S SURE TOMORROW J.H. Blackstone
1. The rapture of the church is the next prophetic event.	The removal of the judgmental blindness that has been on Israel nationally for 1900 years and the offer of salvation to them is the next prophetic event.
2. Jesus had offered Himself as King but was rejected, so postponed the Kingdom.	Jesus refused to be crowned king but was established King by His Father and has been reigning since His resurrection.
3. The Tabernacle of David will be rebuilt after God takes out of the Gentiles a people for His Name.	Jesus has already rebuilt David's fallen house and has been taking out of the Gentiles a people for His Name in the church.
4. Redeemed Israel will not be part of the church.	Since the cross there is salvation only in Christ. All the redeemed are His Body, the church and Israel nationally will become a part of it by grace.

5. God's purpose with Israel is to make her the leading nation of the world.

God's purpose with Israel is to make all Israeli believers part of His church.

6. The Day of Jacob's trouble is still future.

The Day of Jacob's trouble was the time when the nation was destroyed in 67-70 A.D.

7. Daniel's 70th week begins after the rapture.

Daniel's 70th week began with Messiah's public ministry and concluded 3½ years after His cross.

8. Ezekiel's temple will be built in Jerusalem.

Ezekiel's temple may refer to the temple built by the captives returned from Babylon or to Herod's temple, or to the spiritual temple which our Lord is building of "living stones."

9. The Anti-Christ will make a covenant with Israel for one week and by setting himself as god in the temple cause the oblation and sacrifice to cease (Daniel 9:27).

Messiah confirmed a covenant with many during one week and by His sacrifice caused the oblation and sacrifice to cease (Daniel 9:27). The Anti-Christ will fulfill what Paul wrote in II Thessalonians 2.

10. God will still gather the nations against Israel and will defeat her (Zechariah 14:1,2).

God did bring the armies of the Roman Empire and destroyed Jerusalem in 70 A.D. fulfilling Zechariah 14:1,2. I do not believe Israel will be conquered again.

11. Israel will be saved by seeing Jesus when He comes again.

Salvation is not by sight but by faith. Some Israelis have believed but many, many more will yet believe when the judgmental spiritual blindness is removed before the rapture.

12. The converted Jews will be witnesses, winning millions to Christ during the terrible tribulation.

Jews were the first witnesses of the resurrection and turned the world upside down! There can be no salvation after the rapture. Now is the day of salvation.

13. Jesus will reign on earth in a millennial kingdom that will be disrupted by a final revolt of Satan through Gog and Magog.

St. Paul says Jesus is now reigning until all enemies are subject to Him and then He will give the Kingdom to the Father (I Corinthians 15:25).

14. Israel is still God's covenant nation.

The believing remnant of Israel is in the church but unbelieving Israel is still beloved for the fathers' sake though under judgment because of unbelief.

15. Death will still take its toll in the tribulation period and even in the millennium.

Death's power is destroyed at the time of the rapture (I Corinthians 15:24,25).

16. The judgment will take place after the millennium.

The judgment will take place in connection with the second coming of Christ.

Scripture References

Genesis
3:15 - 58
12:2,3,7 - 61
13:15,16 - 62
15:1-21 - 62,63
17:1-22 - 66
17:4,6,7
17:8,9-14 - 157
21:12,13 - 68
22:15-18 - 69
49:8-10 - 86

Exodus
19:3-8 - 123,149
32:9-14 - 74,141
34:6,7 - 96

Leviticus
26:33ff - 98

Numbers
23:21 - 86
24:17-19 - 86
34:1-15 - 64

Deuteronomy
4:25,26,29 - 64
7:6-10 - 140
9:6-8,13,14,23-24 - 141
17:14-20 - 87
32:18,20 - 40,141
32:21 - 32,40,53

Joshua
21:43,45 - 64
23:11-16 - 64

I Samuel
8:4,5,7 - 87

II Samuel
7:16 - 85

I Kings
4:21,24 - 63

Ezra
1:2-4 - 37,100,106,116
7:11-26 - 101,106,118
9:9 - 119

Psalms
2 - 164ff
2:8 - 71,163
69:9 - 117
69:22 - 40
110:1 - 176

Isaiah
1:2-20 - 97,142
6:9,10 - 40,137
9:6,7 - 89,102,162
11:1-16 - 104
13:5 - 95
28:15-18 - 120
40:3,4 - 166
43:7 - 153
52:15 - 131
53:6 - 78
54:1,13 - 105
64:4 - 168

Jeremiah
2:4-13 - 142
3:12-14 - 143
8:18-22 - 143
13:15-17 - 144
15:4 - 101
16:14,15 - 102
29:10 - 74,98
29:18 - 101
31:33-34 - 32,36,79,83,104
31:35-37 - 36

Ezekiel
5:1-17 - 98
6:3-7 - 99
11:19,20 - 105
18:30-32 - 144
23:1-49 - 100
37:1-28 - 102

Daniel
4:37 - 100
9:2 - 108
9:11-14 - 64
9:16-19 - 108
9:24 - 109
9:25-27 - 115ff
12:4 - 113

Hosea
13:9 - 142

Joel
2:28-32 - 163,164

Amos
9:11 - 160

Micah
6:8 - 78

Zechariah
8:23 - 77
9:9,10 - 91,126
12:10-12 - 45,159
13:1 - 160
13:7-14:9 - 167ff
14:1,2 - 79
14:3,4 - 166

Malachai
3:1 - 117
4:5,6 - 156

Matthew
5:17 - 113
8:10-12 - 130
11:14 - 156

13:1-58 - 94,174
17:10-13 - 156
20:25-28 - 91,112,127
21:33-45 - 92,65
21:43 - 92,103
23:35-38 - 78,110,121,137
26:30,31 - 168
27:25 - 78
28:18 - 93,103
28:19 - 165

Mark
3:23-27 - 172
4:12 - 40
14:26,27 - 168

Luke
1:32,33 - 90
1:67-69 - 90
2:10 - 112
12:32 - 92
19:10 - 127
19:41-44 - 145
21:22 - 110
21:24 - 18,65
23:28-31 - 145
24:25,26 - 15,127
24:44,45 - 15

John
1:29 - 111
1:36 - 117
2:13-17 - 117
3:16 - 71
3:30 - 135
4:21,23,24 - 77
4:22 - 74
5:24-29 - 173,174
6:35 - 158
6:45 - 105
8:56 - 70
10:10 - 158
10:11 - 127

10:28 - 157
14:4 - 170
14:27 - 15,158
15:1 - 42,71
16:13 - 15
18:36 - 90
19:15b - 87
19:36,37 - 45,159

Acts
1:3,8-12 - 83,91
1:6-8 - 92
2:16-21 - 163
2:36 - 136
2:38,39 - 60
3:25,26 - 136
4:24-28 - 164
13:32,33,46 - 60,28
15:10,11 - 130
15:15-17 - 161
16:31 - 30
20:25 - 91
28:25-27 - 41
28:28 - 137

Romans
2:28-29 - 15b
3:23 - 28,78
4:9-16 - 68
4:11-13 - 62
5:18,19 - 112
6:14 - 111
8:4 - 134
9:1-5 - 29
9:6-8 - 46,68,84
10:1-21 - 145,31,32,44
11:1 - 39
11:5 - 129
11:12,15 - 41,53
11:23 - 42,51,66
11:25-27 - 18,20,43,44,50,108,148
11:28-33 - 46,47,151
14:17 - 93

15:12 - 103
15:4,9-12,21 - 131
16:25,26 - 132

I Corinthians
2:9,10 - 131,167
15:20-28 - 175
15:25 - 71,93,103,162,165
15:50-54 - 174

II Corinthians
6:2 - 33,47

Galatians
3:7-16 - 38
3:8 - 70,131
3:17,18 - 83,134
3:28,29 - 51,70
4:22-31 - 67
4:27 - 105
6:17 - 173

Ephesians
2:12-22 - 128
2:14-17 - 38,50,127,135
4:4,5 - 170
6:10-12 - 172

Colossians
1:13 - 91,103,172
2:14,15 - 111

I Thessalonians
2:14-16 - 29,78,80,110,164
4:13-17 - 175

II Thessalonians
1:7,8 - 149
1:6-10 - 174
2:11 - 51

II Timothy
3:16 - 14

Hebrews
2:26 - 111

6:13-20 - 59
8:8-13 - 32,74,104,133
9:1-12 - 114
10:19-22 - 115,158
11:19 - 69
11:39,40 - 60
12:22 - 77

I Peter
1:10-12 - 132
1:18,19 - 112
2:8 - 149

II Peter
3:8,9,10 - 152,175,176

I John
2:2 - 112

Revelation
1:7 - 160
1:18 - 111
20:1-9 - 48,172ff
22:10 - 114

Dr. Blackstone was born of missionary parents in Nanking, China, where he spent the first fourteen years of his life. He is a grandson of William E. Blackstone, author of the widely read book, JESUS IS COMING, written in 1878, a book which greatly influenced evangelical Christians to study Bible prophecy.

Dr. Blackstone is a graduate of U.C.L.A. and of Westminster Theological Seminary. He received his M.A. degree from the University of Pittsburg and his Doctor of Divinity from Whitworth College.

In 1944-1946, he served as a Chaplain, USNR assigned first to the Coast Guard 12th Naval District and then to sea duty aboard an attack transport in the Pacific.

Returning to civilian life in 1946, Dr. Blackstone was called to be pastor of the Community Church of Palm Springs, California, where he served faithfully, preaching the Word of God without compromise and shepherding the growing congregation until his retirement in 1974. From 1975 to 1978, he was president of the Conservative Congregational Christian Conference.

During the past fifteen years, he has contributed articles regularly for the devotional magazine, SEEK, published by Good News Publishers.

Throughout his entire ministry, he has studied the Scriptures, especially those concerning the Second Coming of Jesus Christ and the hope of Israel, and presents in this book the result of his study.

The Blackstones have lived in Vista, California, since 1976.

Bibliography

Anderson, Sir Robert—THE COMING PRINCE. Glasgow, Scotland: Pickering and Inglis, 11th edition, n.d.

Beegle, Dewey M.—PROPHECY AND PREDICTION. Ann Arbor, Mich.: Pryor Pettingill, Publisher 1978

Blackstone, W.E.—JESUS IS COMING. New York: Fleming H. Revell Co. 1908

Boettner, Loraine—THE MILLENNIUM. Phillipsburg, N.J.: The Presbyterian and Reformed Publishing Co. 1979

Brooks, Keith L.—PROPHECIES OF THE EPISTLES. Los Angeles, CA: American Prophetic League Inc. 1942

Campbell, Roderick—ISRAEL AND THE NEW COVENANT. Phillipsburg, N.J.: Presbyterian and Reformed Publishing Co. 1954

Carver, Ernest L.—WHEN JESUS COMES AGAIN. Phillipsburg, N.J.: Presbyterian and Reformed Publishing Co. 1979

Cox, William E.—AMILLENNIALISM TODAY. Nutley, N.J.: Presbyterian and Reformed Publishing Co. 1977

DeCaro, Louis A.—ISRAEL TODAY, FULFILLMENT OF PROPHECY? Phillipsburg, N.J.: Presbyterian and Reformed Publishing Co. 1974

DeHaan, M.R.—COMING EVENTS IN PROPHECY. Grand Rapids, Mich.: Zondervan Publishing House 1967

Eban, Abba Solomon—PROMISED LAND. Nashville, Tenn.: Thomas Nelson Inc., Publishers 1978

Feinberg, Charles L.—PREMILLENNIALISM OR AMILLENNIALISM? Wheaton, Ill. Van Kampen Press Inc. 1954

Gaebelein, A.C.—THE PROPHET DANIEL. New York: F.E. Fitch Inc. 1911

Griffith Thomas, W.H.—ST. PAUL'S EPISTLE TO THE ROMANS. Grand Rapids, Mich.: Wm. B. Erdmans Publishing Co. 1947

Gundry, Robert H.—THE CHURCH AND THE TRIBULATION. Grand Rapids, Mich.: The Zondervan Publishing House 1973

Hamilton, Gavin—COMING KINGDOM GLORIES. Edinburgh, Scotland: McCall Barber 1965

Hendriksen, William—MORE THAN CONQUERORS. Grand Rapids, Mich.: Baker Book House 1971

Ironside, H.A.—THE LAMP OF PROPHECY. Grand Rapids, Mich.: Zondervan Publishing House 1971

Jocz, Jakob—THE JEWISH PEOPLE AND JESUS CHRIST. Grand Rapids, Mich.: Baker Book House 1979

Kak, Arthur W.—THE REBIRTH OF THE STATE OF ISRAEL. Chicago, Ill.: Moody Press 1958

Kent, H. Harold—THE UNVEILING OF JESUS CHRIST. Toronto, Canada: G.R. Welch Company, Limited 1978

Lindsay, Hal—THE 1980'S: COUNTDOWN TO ARMAGED-DON. King of Prussia, Pa.: Westgate Press Inc. 1980

Lindsell, Harold—THE GATHERING STORM. Wheaton, Ill.: Tyndale House Publishers 1981

Mauro, Philip—THE GOSPEL OF THE KINGDOM. Swengel, Pa.: Reiner Publications 1978

Moule, H.C.G.—THE EPISTLE TO THE ROMANS. Ft. Washington, Pa.: Christian Literature Crusade 1975

Murray, John—THE EPISTLE TO THE ROMANS. Grand Rapids, Mich.: Wm. B. Erdmans Publishing Co. 1979

Newell, William R.—THE BOOK OF THE REVELATION. Chicago, Ill.: Grace Publications 1945

Scott, Walter—EXPOSITION OF THE REVELATION OF JESUS CHRIST. Westwood, N.J.: Fleming H. Revell Co. Fourth edition n.d.

Snyder, Howard A.—THE COMMUNITY OF THE KING. Downers Grove, Ill.: Inter Varsity Press 1978

Vos, Geerhardus—THE PAULINE ESCHATOLOGY. Princeton, N.J.: Princeton University Press 1930

Walvoord, John F.—THE MILLENNIAL KINGDOM, Grand Rapids, Mich.: Zondervan Publishing House 1959

_____.—ISRAEL IN PROPHECY. Grand Rapids, Mich.: Zondervan Publishing Co. 1970

_____.—THE CHURCH IN PROPHECY. Grand Rapids, Mich.: Zondervan Publishing Co. 1972

_____.—THE NATIONS IN PROPHECY. Grand Rapids, Mich.: Zondervan Publishing House 1972

Wolff, Richard—ISRAEL TODAY. Wheaton, Ill.: Tyndale House Publishers 1970